Birds of Illinois

Field Guide

by Stan Tekiela

ADVENTURE PUBLICATIONS
CAMBRIDGE, MINNESOTA

TO MY WIFE KATHERINE AND DAUGHTER ABIGAIL WITH ALL MY LOVE.

ACKNOWLEDGMENTS:

Special thanks to Anthony Hertzel for range maps, and Illinois birders Jim Phillips, Michael L. P. Retter and Eric Walters for reviewing them.

I would like to thank the technical editors, whose extensive knowledge of birds made this book possible:

Kathy Beaulieu	Deanne Endrizzi	Louise Linnaeus
Brian Collins	Kathy Heidel	Frank Nicoletti
Kim Eckert	Carrol Henderson	George Tkach
Dudley Edmondson	Anthony Hertzel	

Book design and Illustrations by Jonathan Norberg

Photo credits by photographer and page number:
Cover photo: Cedar Waxwing by Dudley Edmondson
Brian Collins: 2, 122, 150, 210, 220, 230 **Cornell Laboratory of Ornithology:** 58, 60 (female), 64, 66 (perching), 192 (both) **Dudley Edmondson:** 16, 42 (soaring), 44, 46 (both), 68, 74, 80, 90 (both), 100, 102, 114 (in flight), 124 (both), 126 (male), 130, 138 (soaring), 154, 156 (both), 168, 172 (male), 182, 188 (male), 194, 196 (both), 200, 202, 236, 238, 248 (male), 250, 252 (male), 258 **Carrol Henderson:** 82 **Kevin T. Karlson:** 34, 116 (female), 244, 254 **Bruce Leventhal:** 242 **Bill Marchel:** 4, 6, 22 (male), 24, 30, 60 (male), 72, 92 (white-striped) 96, 106, 118, 128, 134, 138 (perching), 142, 146, 152 (female), 172 (female), 176, 206, 208 (both), 214, 216, 222, 228, 234, 240 **Maslowski Wildlife Productions:** 20, 62, 76, 98, 110, 162, 164, 170, 184, 232, 246, 256 **Missouri DNR:** 88 **Arthur Morris:** 116 (male) **Steve Mortensen:** 8, 14, 22 (female), 26 (male), 28 (both), 38 (both), 40, 42 (perching), 48, 50, 52, 54 (both), 84, 86 (both), 144, 148, 166, 178, 180, 212, 248 (female), 262 (both) **Warren Nelson:** 10, 26 (female), 66 (in flight), 114 (perching), 126 (female), 252 (female) **John Pennoyer:** 70, 112, 218, 226 **Brian E. Small:** 108 (winter), 136, 224, 260 **Stan Tekiela:** 12, 18 (both), 32 (both), 36, 56 (both), 78, 92 (tan-striped), 94 (both), 104, 108 (breeding), 120, 132, 140, 152 (male), 158, 160, 174, 186, 188 (female), 190, 204, 264 **Brian Wheeler:** 198 (both)

To the best of the publisher's knowledge, all photos but one were of live birds.

Fifth Printing
Copyright 1999 by Stan Tekiela
Published by Adventure Publications, Inc.
820 Cleveland St. S
Cambridge, MN 55008
1-800-678-7006
All rights reserved
Printed in China

TABLE OF CONTENTS
Introduction

WHY WATCH BIRDS IN ILLINOIS?

Millions of people have discovered birdfeeding. It's a simple and enjoyable way to bring the beauty of birds closer to your home. Watching birds at your feeder often leads to a lifetime pursuit of bird identification. The *Birds of Illinois Field Guide* is for those who want to identify the *common birds* of the Land of Lincoln.

There are more than 800 species of birds found in North America. In Illinois alone there have been 420 different kinds of birds recorded over the years. These bird sightings were diligently recorded by thousands of bird watchers and reported to the Illinois Ornithological Society and became part of the official state record. From these valuable records, I have chosen 111 of the most common birds of Illinois to include in this field guide.

Bird watching, often called "birding," is the largest spectator sport in America. Its outstanding popularity in Illinois is due, in part, to an unusually rich and abundant birdlife. Why are there so many birds? First, Illinois is more than 57,900 square miles (150,500 sq. km) in size making it the twenty-fifth largest state. Despite its large size, only about 12 million people call Illinois home! That is only 197 people per square mile (76 per sq. km). Also, 85 percent of all the people in Illinois live in urban settings around the major cities, leaving a lot of open space.

But open space is not the only reason there is such an abundance of birds – it's also the diversity of habitat. The state can be broken into three distinct regions, (north, central and south) each of which supports a different group of birds. Water also plays a big part in Illinois bird populations. The state is bounded on the west by the Mississippi River, and by Lake Michigan and the Wabash River on the East and the Ohio River on the south.

Lake Michigan is a natural funnel for migrating birds since they follow the shoreline avoiding flying over large bodies of water. A gentle northwesterly wind often blows the inland birds up against the shoreline making the lake front along Michigan a good spot for many migrating birds.

The northwestern corner of Illinois has large stands of white birch and rolling hills and is home to birds such as the Chestnut-sided Warbler. It is also a good place to see some of the "winter finches" such as the Purple Finch.

The central portion of the state, which was originally a prairie habitat and is now agricultural, has many open country birds such as the Horned Lark. The rivers of central Illinois are lined with deep rich forest that harbor many birds including many kinds of waterfowl.

Southern Illinois is known for its extensive tracts of forest and winding rivers. The forested valleys and ridges are home for many birds such as the Scarlet Tanager.

Besides the varying habitat, Illinois has varying weather. Since the state extends over 370 miles from north to south, the weather ranges greatly. From the frigid winters of the north to the steamy summers of the south there are birds to watch in every season. Whether witnessing a migration of hawks in the fall or welcoming back the hummingbirds in the spring, there is variety and excitement in birding as each season turns to the next.

OBSERVE WITH A STRATEGY;
TIPS FOR IDENTIFYING BIRDS

Identifying birds isn't as difficult as you might think. If you follow just a few basic strategies, you can increase your chances of successfully identifying most birds you see! One of the first and easiest things to do when you see a new bird is to note its color. (Also, since this book is organized by color, you will go right to that color section to find it.)

Next, note the size of the bird. A strategy to quickly estimate size is to select a small-, medium-, and large-sized bird to use for reference. For example, most people are familiar with robins. A robin, measured from the tip of its bill to the tip of its tail, is 10 inches long. Using the robin as an example of a middle-sized bird, select two other birds, one smaller and one larger. Many people use a House Sparrow, at about 6 inches, and an American Crow, about 18 inches. When you see a bird that you don't know, you can quickly ask yourself "Is it smaller than a robin but larger than a sparrow?" When you look in your field guide to help identify your bird, you'll know it's roughly between 6 and 10 inches long. This will help narrow your choices.

Next, note the size, shape, and color of the bill. Is it long, thin, pointed, short, thick, blunt, curved, or straight? Seed eating birds, such as the Northern Cardinal, have bills that are thick and strong enough to crack even the toughest seeds. Birds that sip nectar, like Ruby-throated Hummingbirds, need long, thin bills to reach deep into flowers. Hawks and owls tear their prey with very sharp, curved bills. Sometimes, just noting the bill shape can help you decide if the bird is a woodpecker, finch, grosbeak, or blackbird.

Next, take a look around and note the habitat in which you see the bird. Is the bird wading in a marsh? Is it walking along a river bank? Soaring in the sky? Is it perched high up in the trees or hopping along on the forest floor? Because of their preferences in diet and habitat, you'll often see robins hopping on the ground but usually not eating the seeds at your feeder. Or you'll see a Rose-breasted Grosbeak sitting on the branches of your tree but not climbing up the trunk of a tree the way a nuthatch does.

Noticing what a bird is eating will give you another clue to help you identify that bird.Feeding is a big part of any bird's life. Fully one-third of all bird activities revolve around searching for and catching food, or actually eating. While birds don't always follow all the "rules" of what we think they eat, you can make some general assumptions. Northern Flickers, for instance, feed upon ants, and other insects, so you wouldn't expect to see them visiting a backyard bird feeder. Some birds, such as the Barn and Tree Swallow, feed on flying insects, and spend hours swooping and diving to catch a meal.

Sometimes you can identify a bird by the way it is perched. Body posture can help you to differentiate between an American

Crow and a Red-tailed Hawk. American Crows lean forward over their feet when perched on a branch, while hawks perch in an upright or vertical position. Look for this the next time you see a large unidentified bird in a tree.

Birds in flight are often difficult to identify, but noting the size and shape of the wing will help. Birds' wings are in direct proportion to their body size, weight, and type of flying. The shape of the wing determines if the bird flies fast and with precision, or slowly and less precisely. Birds such as House Finches, which flit around a thick tangle of branches, have short, round wings. Birds that soar on warm updrafts of air, such as Turkey Vultures, have wings that are long and broad. Barn Swallows have short, pointed wings that slice through the air, propelling their swift and accurate flight.

Some birds have unique flight patterns that will aid in identification. The American Goldfinch flies in a distinctive up and down pattern that makes it look as if it's riding a roller coaster. To tell the difference between an American Crow and a Common Raven, see if it flies with continuous flapping (the American Crow) or interrupts its flapping with periods of soaring (the Common Raven.)

It takes practice to make these observations in just the short time you often have to actually watch a bird. It's not something that comes easily with your very first "mystery bird." Practicing these methods of identification will greatly expand your birding skills. It also helps to seek out the guidance of a more experienced birder who will help you improve your skills and answer your questions on the spot.

BIRD BASICS

It's easier to identify birds and communicate about them if you know the names of the different parts of a bird. For instance, it's much easier to use the word "crest" to describe the erect feathers on the head of a Northern Cardinal than trying to describe it.

The following illustration points out the basic parts of a bird. It is a composite of many birds, and should not be confused with any actual bird.

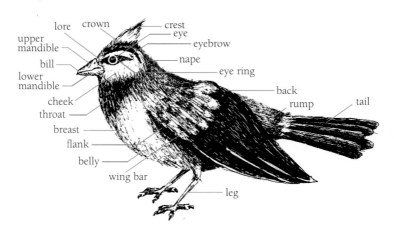

BIRD COLOR VARIABLES

No other animal has a color pallet like a bird's. Vivid blues, lemon yellows, intense reds, and iridescent greens are commonplace within the bird world. In general, male birds are more colorful than their female counterparts. This is probably to help the male attract a mate, essentially saying "Hey, look at me!" It also calls attention to the male's overall health. The better the condition of his feathers, the better his food source and territory, and therefore, the better potential for a mate.

Females that don't look like their male counterparts (such species are called sexually dimorphic, meaning two forms) are often a nondescript brown color, as seen with the Rose-breasted Grosbeak. These muted tones help to hide the females during weeks of motionless incubation, and draw less attention to her when she is out feeding or taking a break from the rigors of raising her young.

In some species, such as the Bald Eagle, Blue Jay, and Woodpecker, the male birds look nearly identical to the females. In the case of the woodpeckers, the sexes are only differentiated by a single red or sometimes yellow mark. Depending on the species, the mark may be on top of the head, face, nape of the neck, or just behind the bill.

During their first year, juvenile birds often look like their mothers. Since brightly colored feathers are used mainly for attracting a mate, young non-breeding males don't have any need for colorful plumage. This also helps protect them while they are young. It is not until the first spring molt, or even several years later, depending on the species, that young males obtain their breeding colors.

MOLTING

All birds molt. Molting is the process of dropping old worn feathers and replacing them with new ones. Typically a bird will molt twice a year, with the first molt, or spring molt, usually occurring in late winter. During this molt the birds produce their breeding plumage (brighter colors for attracting mates), which will carry them through the summer. The second, or summer molt, serves two important functions. First, it adds additional feathers for warmth in the coming winter. Second, the winter plumage tends to be more drab in color, such as that of the male American Goldfinch, which changes from canary yellow to olive brown. Luckily for us, some birds, such as the male Northern Cardinal, retain their bright summer color all year long.

BIRD NESTS

Bird nests are truly an amazing feat of engineering. Just imagine building your home strong enough to weather a storm, large enough to hold your entire family, warm enough to shelter them from the cold, and waterproof enough to keep out rain. Now, build it without any blueprints or directions, and without the use of your hands or feet! Birds do!

Before building a nest, an appropriate site must be selected. With some birds, such as the House Wren, the male picks out several potential sites, and assembles several small twigs in each. This discourages other birds from using nearby nest cavities. These "extra" nests are sometimes called "dummy" nests. The female is then taken around and shown all the choices. She chooses her favorite and finishes constructing the nest. With some other species of birds, for example Baltimore Orioles, it's the female who chooses the site and builds the nest with the male only offering an occasional suggestion. Each bird species has its own nest building routine which is strictly followed.

Nesting material usually consists of natural elements found in the immediate area. Most nests consist of plant fibers (such as bark peeled from grapevines), sticks, mud, dried grass, feathers, fur, or soft fuzzy tufts from thistle. Some birds, including Ruby-throated Hummingbirds, use spider webs to glue nest materials together. Nesting material is limited to what a bird can hold or carry. Because of this, a bird must make many trips afield to gather enough materials to complete its nest. Most nests take at least four days or more, and hundreds, if not thousands, of trips to build.

As you'll see in the following illustrations, birds build a wide variety of nest types.

ground nest   platform nest   cup nest   pendulous nest

The simple **ground nest** is scraped out of the earth. These shallow depressions usually contain no nesting material, and are made by birds such as the Killdeer and Horned Lark.

Another type of nest, the **platform nest**, represents a more complex type of nest building. Constructed of small twigs and branches, the platform nest is a simple arrangement of sticks which forms a platform and features a small depression to nestle the eggs. Some platform nests are constructed on the ground and are made of mud and grass such as that of the Common Loon.

Platform nests can also be on cliffs, bridges, balconies or even in flower pots. This kind of nest gives space to adventurous youngsters, and functions as a landing platform for the parents. Many waterfowl construct platform nests on the ground, usually near water or actually in the water. These floating platform nests vary with the water level, thus preventing nests with eggs from being flooded. Platform nests, constructed by such birds as Mourning Doves and herons, are not anchored to the tree, and may tumble from the branches during high winds and storms.

The **cup nest** is a modified platform nest, used by three-quarters of all songbirds. Constructed from the outside in, a supporting platform is constructed first. This platform is attached firmly to a tree, shrub, or rock ledge. Next, the sides are constructed of grasses, small twigs, bark, or leaves, which are woven together and often glued with mud for additional strength. The inner cup, lined with feathers, animal fur, soft plant material, or animal hair, is constructed last. The mother bird uses her chest to cast the final contours of the inner nest.

The **pendulous nest** is an unusual nest, looking more like a sock hanging from a branch than a nest. Inaccessible to most predators, these nests are attached to the ends of the smallest branches of a tree, and often wave wildly in the breeze. Woven very tightly of plant fibers, they are strong and water tight, taking up to a week to build. More commonly used by tropical birds, orioles and kinglets have mastered this complicated nest type. A small opening on the top or side allows the parents access to the grass lined interior. (It must be one heck of a ride to be inside one of these nests during a windy spring thunderstorm!)

One of the most clever of all nest types is known as the no nest or day care nest. Parasitic birds, like the Brown-headed Cowbird, build no nest at all! The egg-laden female expertly searches out other birds' nests and sneaks in to lay one of her own eggs while the host mother is not looking, thereby leaving the host mother to raise an adopted child. The mother Cowbirds waste no energy building a nest that might only be raided by a predator, and by using several nests of other birds, she spreads out her progeny in the hopes that at least one of her offspring will live to maturity.

Another nest type, the **cavity nest**, is used by many birds, including woodpeckers and Eastern Bluebirds. The cavity nest is usually excavated in a tree branch or trunk, and offers shelter from the storms, sun, predators, and the cold of Illinois' climate. A relatively small entrance hole in a tree leads to an inner chamber up to 10 inches below. In some cases, such as the King Fisher, a four foot tunnel connects the entrance in the bank to the nest chamber. These nests are often sparsely lined, due to the fact that they are so well insulated. Usually constructed by woodpeckers and kingfishers, the cavity nest is used only once by its builder, but can be used for many years by birds such as the Common Goldeneye, mergansers, and bluebirds, that do not have the capability of excavating one for themselves.

Some birds, including some swallows, take nest building one step beyond. They use a collection of small balls of mud, and construct an adobe-style home. Constructed under the eaves of houses, under bridges, or inside chimneys, some of these nests look like simple cup nests, while others are completely enclosed, with small tunnel-like openings that lead into a safe nesting chamber for the baby birds.

WHO BUILDS THE NEST

In general the female bird builds the nest. She will gather nesting materials and construct a nest with only an occasional visit from her mate to look in on the progress. In some species both parents contribute equally to the construction of a nest. A male bird might forage for just the right sticks, grass, or mud for building but it's often the female that forms or puts together the nest. She uses her body to form the egg chamber. Rarely does the male build a nest by himself.

FLEDGING

Fledging is the period or interval between hatching and flight or leaving the nest. While some birds leave the nest within hours of hatching, it might be weeks before they are able to fly. This is common with waterfowl. Until they start to fly they are called fledglings. Birds that are still in the nest are called nestlings.

WHY BIRDS MIGRATE

Why do birds migrate? The short answer is simple–food. Birds migrate to areas of high food concentrations. It is easier to breed where the food is than where it is not. A typical migrating bird, the Rose-breasted Grosbeak for instance, migrates from the tropics of Central and South America to nest in the forests of North America taking advantage of the billions of newly hatched insects to feed its young. This trip is called **complete migration**.

Some birds of prey return from their complete migration to northern regions that are over-flowing with small rodents such as mice and voles that have continued to breed even in winter.

Complete migrators have a set time and pattern of migration. Each year at nearly the same time, they take off and head for a specific wintering ground. Complete migrators may travel incredible distances, sometimes as much as 15,000 miles or more in one year, but complete migration doesn't necessarily imply flying from the cold and frozen northland to some tropical paradise. The Dark-eyed Junco, for example, is a complete migrator that flies from the far reaches of Canada to spend the winter right here in Illinois.

There are many interesting aspects to complete migrators. In the spring, males usually migrate several weeks before the females, arriving early to begin to defend territories and to scope out possible nesting sites, food sources, and begin to defend territories. The females then "catch up" several weeks later. In the autumn, in many species, it's the females and their young that leave early, often up to four weeks before their mates.

Not all migrators are the same. There are **partial migrators**, such as American Goldfinches, that usually wait until food supplies dwindle before they fly south. Unlike complete migrators, the partial migrators move only far enough south, or sometimes east and west, to find abundant food. Some years it might be only a few hundred miles, while other years it might be nearly a thousand. This kind of migration, dependent upon the weather and available food, is sometimes called **seasonal movement**.

Unlike the predictable ebbing and flowing behavior of the complete migrators or partial migrators, **irruptive migrators** can move every third to fifth year, or in some cases in consecutive years. These migrations are triggered when times are really tough and food is scarce. Red-breasted Nuthatches are good examples of irruptive migrators because they leave their normal northern range in search of food or in response to overpopulation.

How Do Birds Migrate?

One of the many secrets of migration is fat. While we humans are fighting the battle of the bulge, birds intentionally gorge themselves to put on as much fat as possible while still being able to fly. Fat provides the greatest amount of energy per unit of weight and, like the gas in your car, they can't go anywhere without it.

During long migratory flights, fat deposits are used up quickly, and birds need to stop to "refuel." This is when backyard bird feeding stations and undeveloped, natural spaces around our towns and cities are especially important. Some birds require up to two to three days of constant feeding to build up their fat reserves again before heading out to continue their seasonal trip.

Some birds, such as most eagles, hawks, osprey, falcons, and vultures, migrate during the day. Larger birds can hold more body fat, go longer without eating, and take longer to migrate. These birds glide along on rising columns of warm air called thermals, which hold them aloft while they slowly make their way south. They generally rest at night and hunt early in the morning before the sun has a chance to warm up the land and create good soaring conditions. Birds migrating during the day use a combination of landforms, rivers, and the rising and setting setting sun to guide them in the right direction.

Most birds migrate during the night. Studies show that birds that migrate at night use the stars to navigate. Others use the setting sun while still others, such as doves, use the earth's magnetic fields to guide them south. While flying at night might seem like a crazy idea, nocturnal migration is safer for several reasons. First, there are fewer nighttime predators for migrating birds. Traveling at night allows time during the day to find food in unfamiliar surroundings. Finally, nighttime wind patterns tend to be flat, or laminar. These flat winds don't have the turbulence associated with daytime winds, and can actually help carry smaller birds by pushing them along.

HOW TO USE THIS GUIDE

To help you quickly and easily identify the birds, this book has been organized by color. Simply note the color of the bird and turn to that section. Refer to the first page for the color key. The Rose-breasted Grosbeak, for example, is black and white with a red patch on its chest. Because the bird is mostly black and white, it will be found in the black and white section. Each color section is arranged by size with the smallest birds being first. Flip through the birds in that color section to find the bird. If you already know the name of the bird, check the index for the page number. In some species, the male and female are remarkably different in color. In these cases, the opposite sex is shown in a smaller inset photograph with a page reference. Therefore these birds will be found in two different color sections.

In the description section you will find a variety of information about the bird. On the following page is a sample of the information included in the book.

RANGE MAPS

Range maps are included for each bird. The colored areas indicate where in Illinois a particular bird is most likely to be found. Green indicates where the bird is likely to be found in the summer, blue in winter, and red all year round. Yellow indicates the bird is seen in these areas during migration. While every effort has been made to accurately depict these ranges, they are only general guidelines. Ranges actually change on an on-going basis due to a variety of factors. Changes in weather, species abundance, landscape and vital resources such as the availability of food and water can affect local populations, migration, and movements, causing birds to be found in areas not typical for the species.

The colored areas simply mean bird sightings for that species have been frequent in those areas and less frequent in the others. Please use the maps as intended—as general guides only.

COMMON NAME
Scientific name

YEAR ROUND
MIGRATION
SUMMER
WINTER

RANGE MAP

Size: measured from head to tail

Male: a brief description of the male bird

Female: a brief description of the female bird, which is sometimes not the same as the male

Juvenile: a brief description of the juvenile bird, which often looks like the female

Nest: the kind of nest this bird builds to raise its young, who builds the nest, and how many broods per year

Eggs: how many eggs you might expect to see in a nest, and the color of the eggs

Incubation: the average time the parents spend incubating the eggs, and who does the incubation

Fledging: the average time the young spend in the nest after hatching but before they leave the nest and which parent(s) does most of the "child-care" and feeding

Migration: type of migration: complete (consistent, seasonal), or partial (seasonal, destination varies), or irruptive (unpredictable, depending on food supply), or non-migrator; general location where the bird spends the winter

Food: what the bird eats most of the time (i.e. seeds, nectar, insects, fruits, small animals), and if it typically comes to a bird feeding station

Compare: notes about other birds that look similar, and the pages on which they can be found

Stan's Notes: Interesting "gee-whiz" natural history information. This could be something to look or listen for, or something to help you positively identify the bird. Also includes remarkable features.

1

female
pg. 98

male

YEAR ROUND
SUMMER

EASTERN TOWHEE
Pipilo erythrophthalmus

Size: 7-8" (18-20 cm)

Male: A mostly black bird with dirty red brown sides and white belly. Long black tail with white tip. Short, stout, pointed bill with rich red eye. White wing patches flash in flight.

Female: similar to male but is brown not black

Juvenile: light brown, heavily-streaked head, chest and belly; long dark tail with white tip

Nest: cup, female builds, 2 brood per year

Eggs: 3-4; creamy white with brown marking

Incubation: 12-13 days, female incubates

Fledging: 10-12 days, female and male feed young

Migration: complete, to southern states and South America

Food: insects, seeds, fruit, will come to ground feeder

Compare: Slightly smaller than the American Robin (pg. 188). Gray Catbird (pg. 186) lacks black hood and rusty sides. Common Grackle (pg. 10) lacks white belly and has a long thin bill. Rose-breasted Grosbeak (pg. 24) has rose red patch in center of chest.

Stan's Notes: Its uncommon name comes from its distinctive "tow-hee" call given by both sexes. Mostly known for its characteristic call that sounds like "drink your tea!" White eyed form in southern states. Seen hopping backward with both feet to rake up the leaf litter, called bilateral scratching, in search of insects and seeds. Female broods, but male does most of the feeding of young.

female pg. 102

male

BROWN-HEADED COWBIRD
Molothrus ater

Size: 7½" (19 cm)

Male: A glossy black bird, reminiscent of a Red-winged Blackbird. Chocolate brown head with a pointed sharp gray bill.

Female: dull brown bird with bill similar to male

Juvenile: similar to female only duller gray with streaked chest

Nest: no nest; lays eggs in nests of other birds

Eggs: 5-7; white with brown markings

Incubation: 10-13 days; host bird incubates eggs

Fledging: 10-11 days; host birds feed young

Migration: complete, to southern states

Food: insects, seeds, will come to seed feeders

Compare: In the blackbird family. The slightly larger Red-winged Blackbird (pg. 8), has red and yellow markings on wings. Common Grackle (pg. 10) has long tail but lacks brown head. European Starling (pg. 6) has yellow bill and shorter tail.

Stan's Notes: Of about 750 species of parasitic birds worldwide, this is the only parasitic bird in Illinois, laying all eggs in "host" birds' nests, leaving others to raise its young. Cowbirds are known to have laid eggs in nests of over 200 species of birds. Some birds reject cowbird eggs, but most raise them, even to the exclusion of their own young. Look for warblers and other birds feeding young birds twice their own size. At one time they followed bison to feed on the insects attracted to the animals.

YEAR ROUND

EUROPEAN STARLING
Sturnus vulgaris

Size: 7½" (19 cm)

Male: An iridescent purple black bird covered with white speckles during fall and winter. Shiny purple black in spring and summer. Long pointed gray bill in autumn and yellow in spring. Short tail.

Female: same as male

Juvenile: similar to adult, only gray brown with streaked chest

Nest: cavity; male and female line cavity; 2 broods per year

Eggs: 4-6; bluish with brown markings

Incubation: 12-14 days; female and male incubate

Fledging: 18-20 days; female and male feed young

Migration: non-migrator to partial migrator, some will move to southern states

Food: insects, seeds, fruit, will come to seed and suet feeders

Compare: Looks similar to Common Grackle (pg. 10), but lacks its long tail.

Stan's Notes: Great songsters, they are also able to mimic sounds. Often displaces woodpeckers, chickadees, and other cavity nesting birds. Can be very aggressive and destroy eggs or young of other birds. The bill changes color with the seasons, yellow in spring and gray in autumn. Jaw is designed to be most powerful when opening, as they pry open crevices to locate hidden insects. Gathers in the hundreds in autumn. Not a native bird, they were introduced to New York City in 1890-91 from Europe.

female pg. 112

male

RED-WINGED BLACKBIRD
Agelaius phoeniceus

Size: 8½" (22 cm)

Male: Jet black bird with red and yellow shoulder patch on upper wing. Pointed black bill.

Female: heavily streaked brown bird with white eyebrow, brown bill

Juvenile: same as female

Nest: cup; female builds; 2-3 broods per year

Eggs: 3-4; bluish green with brown markings

Incubation: 10-12 days; female incubates

Fledging: 11-14 days; female and male feed young

Migration: complete, to southern states, Mexico, and Central America

Food: insects, seeds, will come to seed feeder

Compare: Slightly larger than Brown-headed Cowbird (pg. 8), but less iridescent and lacks Cowbird's brown head. Differs from all blackbirds due to its red and yellow patches on wings called "epaulets."

Stan's Notes: It is a sure sign of spring when the Red-winged Blackbirds return to the marsh. Flocks of up to 100,000 birds have been reported. Males return before females and defend territories. Will repeat call from top of cattail while showing off red and yellow wing bars called epaulets. Nests are usually over shallow water in thick stand of cattails. One of the most widespread and numerous birds in Illinois. Feeds mostly on seeds in spring and fall, switching to insects during summer.

COMMON GRACKLE
Quiscalus quiscula

YEAR ROUND

Size: 11-13" (28-33 cm)

Male: A large, black bird with iridescent blue black head, purple brown body, long black tail, long thin bill, and bright golden eyes.

Female: similar to male only duller and smaller

Juvenile: similar to female

Nest: cup; female builds; 2 broods per year

Eggs: 4-5; greenish white with brown markings

Incubation: 13-14 days; female incubates

Fledging: 16-20 days; female and male feed young

Migration: complete, to southern states

Food: fruits, seeds, insects, will come to seed feeders

Compare: The male Yellow-headed Blackbird is slightly smaller and has a bright yellow head. The European Starling (pg. 6) is much smaller and has a speckled appearance and yellow bill. The Red-winged Blackbird (pg. 8) has red and yellow wing markings.

Stan's Notes: Usually nests in small colonies of up to 75 pair. Travels with other blackbirds in large flocks. Known to feed in farmers' fields. Their name comes from the Latin word "graculus" meaning "to cough" for their loud raspy call. They hold their tail in a keel-like position during flight. Flight pattern is almost always level, as opposed to undulated up and down movements. Unlike most birds, has larger muscles to open mouth rather than to close it, as they pry open crevices to locate hidden insects.

11

AMERICAN COOT
Fulica americana

Size: 13-16" (33-40 cm)

Male: Slate gray to black all over, white bill with dark band near tip. Green legs and feet. Small white patch near base of tail. Prominent red eye and small red patch above bill between eyes.

Female: same as male

Juvenile: much paler than adult, with a gray bill and same white rump patch

Nest: floating platform; female and male build; 1 brood per year

Eggs: 9-12; pinkish buff with brown markings

Incubation: 21-25 days; female and male incubate

Fledging: 49-52 days; female and male feed young

Migration: complete, to southern states and Central America

Food: insects, aquatic plants

Compare: Smaller than most waterfowl, it is the only black water bird or duck-like bird with a white bill.

Stan's Notes: An excellent diver and swimmer often seen in large flocks on open water. Not a duck, as they don't have webbed feet, but instead have large lobed toes. When taking off, they scramble across the surface of the water with wings flapping. Look for them bobbing their heads while swimming. Huge flocks of up to 1,000 birds gather for fall migration. Its unusual name is of unknown origin but in Middle English "coot" was used to describe various waterfowl – perhaps it stuck. Nest is floating mat of vegetation.

13

YEAR ROUND

AMERICAN CROW
Corvus brachyrhynchos

Size: 18" (45cm)

Male: All black bird with black bill, legs, and feet. Can have purple sheen in direct sunlight.

Female: same as male

Juvenile: same as adult

Nest: platform; female builds; 1 brood per year

Eggs: 4-6; bluish to olive green, brown markings

Incubation: 18 days; only female incubates

Fledging: 28-35 days; female and male feed young

Migration: non-migrator to partial migrator

Food: fruits, insects, mammals, fish, carrion, will come to seed and suet feeders

Compare: Similar to Common Raven (rarely seen in Illinois), but has smaller bill and lacks shaggy throat feathers. Has a higher pitched call than the Raven's deep low raspy call. Crow has squared tail. Raven has wedge-shaped tail apparent in flight.

Stan's Notes: One of the most recognizable birds in Illinois. Often reuse nest every year if not taken over by a Great Horned Owl. They collect and store bright, shiny objects in the nest. Able to mimic human voices, and other birds. One of the smartest of all birds, they are very social, often entertaining themselves by provoking chases from other birds. They feed on road kill but are rarely hit by cars. Can live up to 20 years. Unmated birds, known as helpers, help raise young. Large extended families roost together at night then disperse during the day to hunt.

TURKEY VULTURE
Cathartes aura

Size: 26-32" (65-80 cm); up to 6 foot wing span

Male: Large bird with obvious red head and legs. When seen overhead, wings appear two-toned, black leading edge with gray on trailing edge and tip. Tip of wings end in finger-like projections. Squared-off tail. Ivory bill.

Female: same as male

Juvenile: same as adult, but often has a gray to blackish head and bill

Nest: no nest, or minimal nest on cliff or in cave; 1 brood per year

Eggs: 2; white with brown markings

Incubation: 38-41 days; female and male incubate

Fledging: 66-88 days; female and male feed young

Migration: complete, to southern states, Central America, South America

Food: carrion, parents regurgitate for young

Compare: Smaller than Bald Eagle (pg. 46), look for Vulture's two-toned colored wings. Flies holding wings in a slight V-shape compared to the straight wing position of the eagle.

SUMMER
MIGRATION

Stan's Notes: Vultures' naked heads are an adaptation to reduce the risk of feather fouling (picking up diseases) from carcasses. Unlike hawks and eagles, they have weak feet more suited to walking than grasping. One of the few birds with a developed sense of smell. They're generally mute, making only grunts or groans. Groups often seen in trees with wings outstretched to catch sun.

drying

DOUBLE-CRESTED CORMORANT
Phalacrocorax auritus

YEAR ROUND
MIGRATION
SUMMER
WINTER

Size: 33" (83 cm)

Male: Large all black water bird with long snake-like neck. Long yellow orange bill with hooked tip.

Female: same as male

Juvenile: lighter brown with grayish colored neck and breast

Nest: platform nest in colony; male and female build; 1 brood per year

Eggs: 3-4; bluish white, unmarked

Incubation: 25-29 days; female and male incubate

Fledging: 37-42 days; male and female feed young

Migration: complete, to southern states, Mexico, Central America

Food: small fish, aquatic insects

Compare: Same size as Loon (pg. 44), but Cormorant has longer neck and yellow bill, lacking black and white checker pattern of Loon.

Stan's Notes: Often seen flying in large V-formation. Often roost in large groups in trees near water. Catches fish by swimming with wings held at its side. To dry off they strike an erect pose with wings outstretched facing the sun. Their name refers to the nearly invisible crest on their heads. Cormorant comes from the Latin word "corvus," meaning "crow" and "L. marinus," meaning "pertaining to the sea." Literally, "Sea Crow."

MIGRATION
SUMMER

BLACK-AND-WHITE WARBLER
Mniotilta varia

Size: 5" (13 cm)

Male: Striped like a zebra, this small warbler has a white belly and black chin with distinctive black-and-white stripes on crown and black cheek patch.

Female: same as male, only duller and without the black chin and cheek patch

Juvenile: similar to female

Nest: cup; female builds; 1 brood per year

Eggs: 4-5; white with brown markings

Incubation: 10-11 days; female incubates

Fledging: 9-12 days; female and male feed young

Migration: complete, to Central and South America

Food: insects

Compare: Similar to Blackpoll Warbler, which has a solid black patch on head. Watch for it creeping down a tree trunk like a White-breasted Nuthatch (pg. 176). Brown Creeper (pg. 64) is brown and white with a white chest and belly. Creeper's bill is longer and curved downward.

Stan's Notes: One of the first warblers to return each spring. Look for this common warbler searching for insect eggs in the bark of large trees. The female will perform a distraction dance to draw predators away from nest. It is the only warbler that moves head first down a tree trunk. Song sounds like a slowly turning squeaky wheel. Makes nest on the ground concealed under dead leaves.

male

female

DOWNY WOODPECKER
Picoides pubescens

YEAR ROUND

Size: 6" (16 cm)

Male: A small woodpecker with all white belly, black-and-white spotted wings, a black line running through its eyes, a short black bill, a white stripe down back, and a red mark on nape of neck. Several small black spots along side of white tail.

Female: same as male, lacking red mark on nape

Juvenile: same as female, some juveniles can have a red mark near forehead

Nest: cavity; male and female excavate cavity; 1 brood per year

Eggs: 3-5; white, unmarked

Incubation: 11-12 days; female incubates during day, male incubates at night

Fledging: 20-25 days; male and female feed young

Migration: non-migrator

Food: insects, will come to seed and suet feeders

Compare: Almost identical to Hairy Woodpecker (pg. 28), but smaller. Look for shorter, thinner bill of Downy to differentiate them.

Stan's Notes: Both sexes will "drum" on a hollow log or branch to announce territories. Males perform most brooding and incubate all night. One of the most abundant woodpeckers. Small percentage of young will have a red spot on crown. Stiff tail feathers help brace the bird, like a tripod, as it clings to a tree branch. All woodpeckers have long barbed tongues used to pull insects out of tiny places. Will winter roost in cavity.

female
pg. 106

male

MIGRATION
SUMMER

ROSE-BREASTED GROSBEAK
Pheucticus ludovicianus

Size: 7-8" (18-20 cm)

Male: Plump, black-and-white bird with large rose triangular patch on center of chest. Wing linings are rosy red. Large ivory bill.

Female: heavily streaked brown and white with large white eyebrow line, wing linings are orange yellow

Juvenile: same as female

Nest: cup; female and male build; 1-2 broods per year

Eggs: 3-5; blue green with brown markings

Incubation: 13-14 days; female and male incubate

Fledging: 9-12 days; female and male feed young

Migration: complete, to Mexico, Central and South America

Food: insects, seeds, fruit, comes to seed feeders

Compare: Males are very distinctive with no look-alikes. Females look like large sparrows. Female is larger and has more distinctive eyebrow mark than female Purple Finch (pg. 84). Female House Finch (pg. 70) has no eyebrow mark.

Stan's Notes: Both males and females sing, but males sing much louder and clearer. Rich robin-like song. White wing patches flash when in flight. The name "Grosbeak" refers to its large bill used to crush seeds. The male's red breast patch varies in size and shape in each individual. Males arrive first in spring joined by females several days later. Late to arrive in spring and early to leave in autumn.

male

female

YELLOW-BELLIED SAPSUCKER
Sphyrapicus varius

WINTER

Size:	8-9" (20-23 cm)
Male:	Medium-sized woodpecker with checkered back. Has a red forehead, crown and chin. Tan to yellow chest and belly. White wing patches flash while flying.
Female:	similar to male, white marking on chin
Juvenile:	similar to adult, dull brown and lacks any red marking
Nest:	cavity; female and male excavate; 1 brood per year
Eggs:	5-6; white, unmarked
Incubation:	12-13 days; female and male incubate, males incubate during the night, females during the day.
Fledging:	25-29 days; female and male feed young
Migration:	complete, to Mexico and Central America
Food:	insects, tree sap
Compare:	Similar to other woodpeckers, but the male is the only Illinois woodpecker with a red chin patch, female has white chin.

Stan's Notes: Drills holes in a pattern of horizontal rows in small- to medium-sized trees to "bleed" tree sap. Many birds drink from sapsucker taps. Oozing sap also attracts insects which the sapsucker eats. Sapsuckers will defend their sapping sites from other birds. They don't "suck" sap, rather lap with their long tongue. A quiet bird with few vocalizations, but will meow like a cat. Unlike other woodpeckers, drumming rhythm is irregular.

male

female

HAIRY WOODPECKER
Picoides villosus

YEAR ROUND

Size: 9" (23 cm)

Male: A black-and-white woodpecker with a white belly and black wings with rows of white spots. White stripe down back. Long black bill. Red mark on back of head.

Female: same as male, lacks red spot

Juvenile: grayer version of adult, lacks red spot

Nest: cavity; female and male excavate hole; 1 brood per year

Eggs: 3-6; white, unmarked

Incubation: 11-15 days; female and male incubate, female during day, male at night.

Fledging: 28-30 days; male and female feed young

Migration: non-migrator

Food: insects, seeds, nuts, will come to seed and suet feeders

Compare: Larger than Downy Woodpecker (pg. 22), Hairy has a longer bill and lacks Downy's black spots along tail.

Stan's Notes: A common backyard bird that announces its arrival with a sharp chirp before landing on feeders. Has tiny bristle-like feathers at base of bill to protect nostrils from wood dust. Barbed tongue helps extract insects from trees. Drums on hollow logs, branches, or stove pipes in spring to announce territory. Responsible for eating many destructive forest insects. Often prefers to excavate nest cavities in live aspen trees. Has a large more oval-shaped cavity entrance than that of Downy Woodpecker.

YEAR ROUND
SUMMER

RED-HEADED WOODPECKER
Melanerpes erythrocephalus

Size: 9" (23 cm)

Male: The only Illinois woodpecker with an entirely red head. Solid black back, white rump, chest and belly. Has large white patches on wings that flash when in flight. Black tail. Gray legs and bill.

Female: same as male

Juvenile: gray brown with white chest, lacking any red

Nest: cavity; male builds with help from female; 1 brood per year

Eggs: 4-5; white, unmarked

Incubation: 12-13 days; female and male incubate

Fledging: 27-30 days; female and male feed young

Migration: partial migrator, moves around to areas with abundant supply of nuts

Food: insects, fruit, nuts, comes to seed and suet feeders

Compare: No other Illinois woodpecker has an all red head. Pileated Woodpecker (pg. 38) is the only other woodpecker with solid black back and partial red head.

Stan's Notes: Bill is not as well adapted to excavating holes as in other woodpeckers, so it chooses dead or rotten tree branches for nest. Later nesting than the closely related Red-bellied Woodpecker, and will often take over its nest cavity. Prefers more open or edge woodlands with many dead trees. Often seen perching on tops of dead snags. Stores acorns and other nuts.

31

male

female

YEAR ROUND

RED-BELLIED WOODPECKER
Melanerpes carolinus

Size: 9¼" (24 cm)

Male: "Zebra-backed" woodpecker with a white rump. Red crown extends down the nape of neck. Tan breast with a tinge of red on belly which is often hard to see.

Female: same as male, with gray crown

Juvenile: gray version of adult, no red crown or nape

Nest: cavity; female and male build; 1 brood per year

Eggs: 4-5; white, unmarked

Incubation: 12-14 days; male incubates at night and female during the day

Fledging: 24-27 days; female and male feed young

Migration: non-migrator

Food: insects, nuts, fruit, will come to seed and suet feeders

Compare: Similar to Northern Flicker (pg. 126) and Yellow-bellied Sapsucker (pg. 26). Note tan chest and belly with obvious stripes on back. The Red-headed Woodpecker (pg. 31) has an all-red head.

Stan's Notes: Mostly a bird of shady woodlands, it excavates holes in rotten wood looking for spiders, centipedes, and beetles. Often kicked out of nest hole by European Starlings. Will return to same tree to excavate a new nest below that of previous year. Will hammer acorns and berries into crevices of trees for winter food.

male

female pg. 136

LESSER SCAUP
Aythya affinis

MIGRATION
WINTER

Size: 16-17" (41-43 cm)

Male: Appears mostly black with bold white sides and gray back. Chest and head look nearly black but in sun, head appears purple with green highlights. Bright yellow eye.

Female: overall brown with a dull white patch near base of bill

Juvenile: same as female

Nest: ground; female builds; 1 brood per year

Eggs: 8-14; olive buff without markings

Incubation: 22-28 days, female incubates

Fledging: 45-50 days, female teaches young what to feed on

Migration: complete, to the southern states, northern South America, Central America

Food: aquatic plants and insects

Compare: Nearly identical to the slightly larger but much more uncommon Greater Scaup. Larger than Blue-winged Teal (pg. 134), male Blue-winged Teal has a bright white crescent shape patch near base of bill.

Stan's Notes: Probably one of the most common of all the diving ducks in Illinois. Often seen in large flocks numbering in the thousands on area lakes, ponds and sewage lagoons. Mostly seen during spring and fall migration. When seen in flight note bold white stripe on the wings. Has an interesting babysitting arrangement. where young form groups tended by 1-3 adult females.

female pg. 140

male

HOODED MERGANSER
Lophodytes cucullatus

Size: 16-19" (40-48 cm)

Male: Sleek black-and-white bird with rusty brown sides. Crest "hood" raises to reveal large white patch. Long thin black bill.

Female: sleek brown and rust bird with a ragged rusty crest and long, thin brown bill

Juvenile: similar to female

Nest: cavity; female lines former woodpecker hole; 1 brood per year

Eggs: 10-12; white, unmarked

Incubation: 32-33 days; female incubates

Fledging: 71 days; female feeds young

Migration: complete, to gulf coast, Mexico

Food: small fish, aquatic insects

Compare: Smaller than Common Merganser (pg. 216). Look for large white patch on "hood" and rusty sides.

Stan's Notes: Not as common as the Common Merganser, the male Hooded Merganser can voluntarily raise and lower the crest on its head to show off the large white patch. Females will "dump" eggs into other female Hooded Mergansers' nests resulting in 20-25 eggs in some nests. Mergansers have been known to share a nesting cavity with Goldeneyes and Wood Ducks sitting side by side.

male

female

YEAR ROUND

PILEATED WOODPECKER
Dryocopus pileatus

Size: 19" (48 cm)

Male: Large crow-sized black-backed woodpecker with bright red crest on head. Long gray bill with red mustache. Leading edge of wings white, flashing brightly when flying.

Female: same as male, but has a black forehead and lacks red mustache

Juvenile: similar to adults, only duller and browner overall

Nest: cavity; male and female excavate; 1 brood per year

Eggs: 3-5; white, unmarked

Incubation: 15-18 days; female and male incubate, male incubates at night, female during the day

Fledging: 26-28 days; female and male feed young

Migration: non-migrator

Food: insects, suet, will come to suet feeders

Compare: The Red-headed Woodpecker (pg. 30) is about half the size and has all red head, black back, and white rump.

Stan's Notes: Our largest woodpecker, it excavates long oval holes, up to several feet long, in tree trunks in search of insects. Large chips of wood lay at the base of excavated trees. Will drum on hollow branches, chimneys, etc. to announce its territory. Relatively shy bird that prefers large tracts of woodlands. Young are fed regurgitated insects. Favorite food is carpenter ants.

male

female pg. 144

WINTER

COMMON GOLDENEYE
Bucephala clangula

Size: 18½-20" (47-50 cm)

Male: A mostly white duck with a black back, a large puffy green head, and a large white spot in front of each bright golden eye.

Female: mostly gray with a white collar, a large dark brown head, and bright golden eyes

Juvenile: same as female

Nest: cavity; female lines former woodpecker cavity; 1 brood per year

Eggs: 8-10; light green without markings

Incubation: 28-32 days; female incubates

Fledging: 56-59 days; female leads young to food

Migration: complete, to southern states

Food: aquatic plants, insects

Compare: Similar to, but larger than the black and white Lesser Scaup (pg. 34). Look for distinctive white mark in front of its golden eye and white chest.

Stan's Notes: Known for their loud whistling, which is produced by their wings in flight. In spring, males often attract females through elaborate displays, throwing their head backwards while uttering a single raspy note. Females will lay eggs in other Goldeneye nests, resulting in some mothers incubating up to 30 eggs. Received its common name from its obvious bright golden eyes.

soaring

OSPREY
Pandion haliaetus

MIGRATION

Size: 24" (60 cm); up to 5-6 foot wing span

Male: Large eagle-like bird with white belly and black brown back. Large wings angled (cocked) backwards with black "wrist" marks. White head with a black streak across eyes.

Female: same as male

Juvenile: same as adult

Nest: platform; female and male build; 1 brood per year

Eggs: 2-4; white, with brown markings

Incubation: 32-42 days; female and male incubate

Fledging: 48-58 days; male and female feed young

Migration: complete, to Mexico, Central and South America

Food: fish

Compare: Bald Eagle (pg. 46) is nearly 10 inches larger and has all white head and tail. Immature Bald Eagle is all brown with white speckles. Look for a white belly and dark stripe across eye to identify Osprey.

Stan's Notes: Osprey are in a family all their own. It is the only raptor that will plunge into the water to catch fish. Look for its angulated wings while in flight. Nests on man-made towers and tall dead trees. Can hover for a few seconds before diving. Carries fish in a head first position during flight for better aerodynamics. Recent studies show that male and female might mate for life but don't migrate to the same wintering grounds.

43

COMMON LOON
Gavia immer

Size: 28-36" (70-90 cm)

Male: Large, familiar black-and-white bird of the lakes. Checkerboard back with white necklace, black head, deep red eye, and long pointed black bill in summer and gray in fall and winter.

Female: same as male

Juvenile: gray version of adult, without red eye

Nest: platform; female and male build; 1 brood per year

Eggs: 2; olive brown, occasionally brown markings

Incubation: 26-31 days; female and male incubate

Fledging: 75-80 days; female and male feed young

Migration: complete, to Gulf coast, southern states, and Mexico

Food: fish, aquatic insects

Compare: The Double-Crested Cormorant (pg. 18) has a yellow bill and black chest.

Stan's Notes: A true symbol of the wildness of our lakes. Prefers clear lakes because it hunts for fish by eyesight. Legs are set so far back that it has a hard time walking on land but it's a great swimmer. Its name comes from the Swedish word "lom," meaning "lame" for the awkward way it walks on land. Its unique call suggests the wild laughter of a demented person, and led to the phrase "crazy as a loon." Young ride on the backs of swimming parents. Adults will perform distraction display to protect young. Very sensitive to disturbance during nesting and will abandon nest.

soaring

BALD EAGLE
Haliaeetus leucocephalus

YEAR ROUND
MIGRATION
WINTER

Size: 31-37" (79-94 cm); up to 7 foot wing span

Male: Dark brown to black body and wings set off by pure white head and tail. Large, curved yellow bill and yellow feet.

Female: same as male, only slightly larger

Juvenile: dark brown with white spots or speckles throughout its body and wings, gray bill

Nest: massive platform; female and male build; 1 brood per year

Eggs: 2; off white, unmarked

Incubation: 34-36 days; female and male incubate

Fledging: 75-90 days; female and male feed young

Migration: partial migrator to southeastern states

Food: fish, carrion, ducks

Compare: Larger than Turkey Vulture (pg. 16). Mature eagle has white head and tail. Turkey Vulture has two-toned wings and flies with wings in a V-shape compared to straight-out wing position of eagle.

Stan's Notes: Often seen soaring, this bird is making a comeback in Illinois. Juveniles attain white head and tail at about 4-5 years of age. For mid-air mating ritual, one bird flips upside down, locking talons with another. Both tumble until they break apart to continue flying. Returns to same nest every year adding sticks, enlarging it to massive proportions, at times up to 1,000 pounds. Thought to mate for life, but will switch mates if not successful reproducing.

TREE SWALLOW
Tachycineta bicolor

SUMMER

Size: 5-6" (13-15 cm)

Male: Blue green in spring and greener in fall. Appears to change color in direct sunlight. White belly, notched tail, and pointed wing tips.

Female: similar to male, duller

Juvenile: gray brown with white belly and grayish breast band

Nest: cavity; female and male line former woodpecker cavity or nest box; 1 brood per year

Eggs: 4-6; white, unmarked

Incubation: 13-16 days; female incubates

Fledging: 20-24 days; female and male feed young

Migration: complete, to Mexico and Central America

Food: insects

Compare: Similar color to Purple Martin (pg. 56) but smaller and has white chest and belly. Barn Swallow (pg. 52) has rust belly and deeply forked tail.

Stan's Notes: The first swallow to return each spring. Easily attracted to your yard with a nest box. Competes with Eastern Bluebirds for nest boxes. Travels great distances to find dropped feathers to line its grass nest. Sometimes seen playing by chasing after dropped feathers. Often seen flying back and forth across open fields feeding on insects. Gathers in large flocks to migrate.

female pg. 82

male

SUMMER

INDIGO BUNTING
Passerina cyanea

Size: 5½" (14 cm)

Male: Vibrant blue finch-like bird. Scattered dark markings on wings and tail.

Female: light brown bird with faint markings

Juvenile: similar to female

Nest: cup; female builds; 2 broods per year

Eggs: 3-4; pale blue, unmarked

Incubation: 12-13 days; female incubates

Fledging: 10-11 days; female feeds young

Migration: complete, to Mexico, Central America and South America

Food: insects, seeds, fruit, will visit seed feeders

Compare: Smaller than Eastern Bluebird (pg. 54) and lacking Bluebird's red chest patch.

Stan's Notes: Usually only the males are noticed. Will come to feeders in spring before insects are plentiful. Like Blue Jays, they don't have any blue pigment in their feathers. Actually a black bird, the sunlight is refracted within the structure of the feather, making them only appear blue. Appears iridescent in direct sunlight. Mostly seen along woodland edges feeding on insects. Males often sing from tree tops to attract mates. A late migrant, with males returning before females and juveniles. Males nearly always return to previous year's nest site. Juveniles move to within a mile from birth site. Migrate at night in flocks of 5-10 birds. Molts to acquire body feathers with gray tips, which quickly wear off to reveal bright blue plumage.

BARN SWALLOW
Hirundo rustica

SUMMER

Size: 7" (18 cm)

Male: A sleek swallow with a blue black back, cinnamon belly, and reddish brown chin. White spots on long forked tail.

Female: same as male, only slightly duller

Juvenile: similar to adults with tan belly and chin and shorter tail

Nest: cup; female and male build; 2 broods per year

Eggs: 4-5; white with brown markings

Incubation: 13-17 days; female incubates

Fledging: 18-23 days; female and male feed young

Migration: complete, to South America

Food: insects, prefers beetles, wasps, and flies

Compare: Cliff Swallow has brown rump and nearly square tail. Tree Swallow (pg. 48) has white belly and chin with only a notched tail. Chimney Swift (pg. 66) has narrow pointed tail with wings longer than body. Purple Martin (pg. 56) is nearly two inches larger and has a dark purple belly.

Stan's Notes: Of the six swallow species in Illinois, this is the only one with a deeply forked tail. Unlike other swallows, the Barn Swallow rarely glides in flight so look for continuous flapping. It builds mud nests using up to 1,000 beak-loads of mud, often in or on barns. Nests in colonies of 4-6 but nesting alone is not uncommon. They drink while flying by skimming water or getting water from wet leaves. They also bathe while flying through rain or sprinklers.

male

female

EASTERN BLUEBIRD
Sialia sialis

YEAR ROUND
SUMMER

Size: 7" (18 cm)

Male: Reminiscent of its larger cousin the American Robin with a rusty red breast and white belly. Sky blue head, back, and tail.

Female: shares rusty red breast and white belly, but is grayer with faint blue tail and wings

Juvenile: similar to female with spots on chest, blue wing markings

Nest: cavity; old woodpecker cavity, or man-made nest box; female builds; 2 broods per year

Eggs: 4-5; pale blue, unmarked

Incubation: 12-14 days; female incubates

Fledging: 15-18 days; male and female feed young

Migration: complete, to southern states

Food: insects, fruit

Compare: Indigo Bunting (pg. 50) is nearly all blue, lacking rusty red chest. Blue Jay (pg. 58) is considerably larger with crest and white markings.

Stan's Notes: Once nearly eliminated from Illinois due to a lack of nesting cavities, bluebirds have made a remarkable comeback with the aid of bird enthusiasts who have put up thousands of bluebird boxes. Easily tamed, they will come to a shallow dish with mealworms in it. Perches on tree or fence post and waits for grasshoppers. Young of first brood will help raise young of second. Gathers in large family groups to migrate. Males return first in spring, followed by females a week or two later.

male

female

PURPLE MARTIN
Progne subis

Size: 8½" (21 cm)

Male: Large swallow-shaped bird, purple head, back and belly. Black wings and tail. Notched tail.

Female: gray purple head and back with a whitish belly, darker wings, and tail

Juvenile: same as female

Nest: cavity; female and male line cavity of house; 1 brood per year

Eggs: 4-5, white, unmarked

Incubation: 15-18 days; female incubates

Fledging: 26-30 days; male and female feed young

Migration: complete, to South America

Food: insects

Compare: The male is the only dark purple bellied swallow. Usually only seen in groups.

Stan's Notes: The largest swallows in North America. Formerly nested in tree cavities but now exclusively nest in man-made nest boxes in Illinois. Their main diet consists of dragonflies, not mosquitoes as once thought. Often drink and bathe while flying by skimming water or flying through rain. Return to same nest site each year. Males arrive before females and yearlings. Often nest within 100 feet of a human dwelling and in fact, the most successful colonies are located within this distance. Young strike out to form new colonies. Huge colonies gather in autumn to migrate to South America.

YEAR ROUND

BLUE JAY
Cyanocitta cristata

Size: 12" (30 cm)

Male: A large bright light blue and white bird with a black necklace. Crest on head moves up and down at will. Gray belly with white face. White wing bars on blue wing. Blue tail with black spots and white tip.

Female: same as male

Juvenile: same as adult, only duller

Nest: cup; female and male build; 1-2 broods per year

Eggs: 4-5; green to blue with brown marks

Incubation: 16-18 days; female incubates

Fledging: 17-21 days; female and male feed young

Migration: non-migrator to partial migrator, moves around to find abundant food source

Food: insects, fruit, carrion, seeds, nuts, attracted to seed feeders

Compare: The Eastern Bluebird (pg. 54) is much smaller and lacks the crest. Belted Kingfisher (pg. 60) lacks the vivid blue color and black necklace of the Blue Jay.

Stan's Notes: One of the few birds to cache food. Will scream like a hawk to scatter birds at a feeder before approaching. Feathers don't have blue pigment, refracted sunlight casts blue light. Known as the alarm of the forest, screaming at any intruders in the woods. Is known to eat eggs or young birds from the nest of other birds.

male

female

BELTED KINGFISHER
Ceryle alcyon

YEAR ROUND

Size:	13" (33 cm)
Male:	Large blue gray bird with white belly. Broad blue gray breast band and a ragged crest that can be raised and lowered at will. Large head with long thick black bill. Small white spot directly in front of red brown eye. Wing tips black with splashes of white that flash when flying.
Female:	same as male but has an additional rusty breast band and flank
Juvenile:	same as adult
Nest:	cavity; female and male excavate; 1 brood per year
Eggs:	6-7; white, unmarked
Incubation:	23-24 days; female and male incubate
Fledging:	23-24 days; female and male feed young
Migration:	complete, to southern states, Central and South America
Food:	small fish
Compare:	Similar in size to Blue Jay (pg. 58), but Kingfisher is darker blue with larger more ragged crest.

Stan's Notes: Seen perched on branches near water, it dives head-first for small fish and returns to branch to eat. Has a loud machine gun-like call. Excavates a deep cavity in bank of river or lake. Parents drop dead fish into water, teaching young to dive. Regurgitates pellets of bones after meals, being unable to pass bones through digestive tract. Mates recognize each other by call.

MIGRATION

CHESTNUT-SIDED WARBLER
Dendroica pensylvanica

Size: 5" (13 cm)

Male: A colorful combination of a yellow cap, black mask set against a white face, chin, chest, and belly. Two yellow wing bars. Chestnut-colored flanks. Gray wings.

Female: similar to male, but flanks duller brown

Juvenile: similar to female, lime green head and back, white eye ring and bright yellow wing bars, lacks chestnut sides

Nest: cup; female builds; 1 brood per year

Eggs: 3-5; white with brown markings

Incubation: 12-13 days; only female incubates

Fledging: 10-12 days; female and male feed young

Migration: complete, to Central America

Food: insects, berries

Compare: Shares a yellow cap with the Yellow-rumped Warbler (pg. 172), but lacks the yellow sides and rump. The Yellow Warbler (pg. 252) is nearly all yellow and lacks the the Chestnut's white chest and chestnut colored flanks.

Stan's Notes: Prefers young open aspen forest, look for this attractive warbler in the spring hopping high in the branches while it hunts for insects. You will usually only get a glimpse of this fast-moving warbler. Will hold its tail in a uplifted position showing white tail. Not uncommon for this bird to approach humans in defense of a nest site.

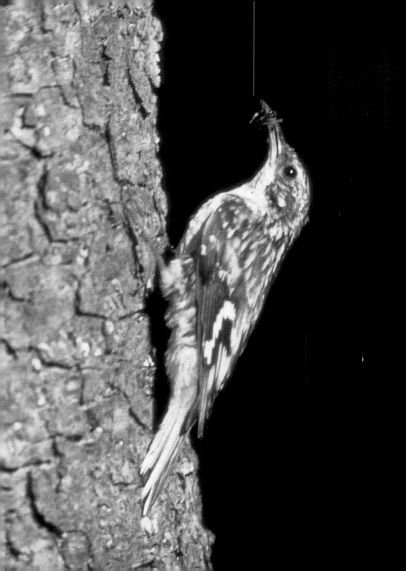

BROWN CREEPER
Certhia americana

YEAR ROUND
WINTER

Size: 5" (13 cm)

Male: A small, thin, nearly camouflaged bird with white belly, long stiff tail, and thin curved bill. Obvious white line above dark eye.

Female: same as male

Juvenile: same as adult

Nest: cup; female builds; unknown how many broods per year

Eggs: 5-6; white with tiny brown markings

Incubation: 14-17 days; only female incubates, male feeds female during incubation

Fledging: 13-16 days; female and male feed young

Migration: partial migrator

Food: insects, nuts, seeds

Compare: "Creeps" up, not down, tree trunks much like the White-breasted Nuthatch (pg. 176). Watch for the Creeper to fly from the top of one trunk to the bottom of another, working its way to the top looking for insects. Slightly larger than Red-breasted Nuthatch (pg. 166), with similar white mark above eye, but Creeper has white belly, long tail, and no black crown.

Stan's Notes: Utilizes camouflage coloring to defend itself by spreading out flat on a branch or trunk without moving. The young are able to follow parents "creeping" soon after fledging. Commonly seen in wooded areas. Often builds nest behind loose bark of dead or dying trees.

65

CHIMNEY SWIFT
Chaetura pelagica

Size: 5" (13 cm)

Male: A nondescript, all brown swallow-shaped bird, usually only seen flying. Long, thin body with pointed tail and head. Long swept back wings are longer than body.

Female: same as male

Juvenile: same as adult

Nest: half cup; female and male build; one brood per year

Eggs: 4-5; white, unmarked

Incubation: 19-21 days; female and male incubate

Fledging: 28-30 days; female and male feed young

Migration: complete, to South America

Food: insects

Compare: Considerably smaller than Purple Martin (pg. 56), and lacks Martin's iridescent purple color. Barn Swallow (pg. 52) has forked tail compared to pointed tail of Chimney Swift. Tree Swallow (pg. 48) has white belly and blue green back.

Stan's Notes: Often called the "flying cigar" due to its pointed body shape. Spends all day flying, rarely perching. They bathe and drink by skimming across water surfaces. Hundreds nest and roost in large chimneys, hence the common name. One of the fastest flyers in the bird world. Unique in-flight twittering call is often heard before bird is seen. Fly in groups, feeding on flying insects nearly 100 feet in the air. Nest made of tiny twigs is cemented with saliva and attached to inside of chimneys or hollow trees.

SUMMER

CHIPPING SPARROW
Spizella passerina

Size: 5" (13 cm)

Male: A small, gray brown sparrow with a clear gray chest, rusty crown, white eyebrow with a black eye line, a thin gray black bill, and two faint wing bars.

Female: same as male

Juvenile: similar to adult, but has streaked chest and lacks rusty cap

Nest: cup; female builds; 2 broods per year

Eggs: 3-5; blue green with brown markings

Incubation: 11-14 days; only female incubates

Fledging: 10-12 days; female and male feed young

Migration: complete, to southern states, Central America, and Mexico

Food: insects, seeds, will come to ground feeders

Compare: Similar to American Tree Sparrow (pg. 86), which shares the rusty crown but American Tree Sparrow lacks dark eye stripe. Look for clear gray chest of Chipping Sparrow. Two inches smaller than the rusty Fox Sparrow (pg. 96).

Stan's Notes: Common garden or yard bird often seen feeding below feeders on dropped seeds. Gathers in large family groups to feed each autumn in preparation for migration. Nest is placed low in dense shrubs and is almost always lined with animal hair. Often just called "chippy." Received its common name from the male's slow "chip" call. Migrates at night in flocks of 20-30 birds.

female

male pg. 226

HOUSE FINCH
Carpodacus mexicanus

Size: 5" (13 cm)

Female: A plain brown bird, with heavily streaked white chest.

Male: orange red face, chest, and rump, with a dark brown marking behind eye, brown wings streaked with white, white belly with brown streaks, brown cap

Juvenile: same as female

Nest: cup; sometimes in cavities; female builds; 2 broods per year

Eggs: 4-5; pale blue, lightly marked

Incubation: 12-14 days; female incubates

Fledging: 15-19 days; female and male feed young

Migration: non-migrator to partial migrator, moves around to find food

Food: seeds, fruit, leaf buds, attract with seed feeder

Compare: Very similar to female Purple Finch (pg. 84). Lacking Purple Finch's bold white eyebrow. Female American Goldfinch (pg. 248) has clear chest and white wing bars. Very similar to Pine Siskin (pg. 74) but without Siskin's yellow on wings.

Stan's Notes: A relatively new bird to Illinois, it was originally introduced to Long Island, New York in the 1940s from western America. A very social bird, it visits feeders in small flocks. Seems to prefer nesting in hanging flower baskets. Incubating female is fed by male. Loud and cheerful warbling song.

71

SUMMER

HOUSE WREN
Troglodytes aedon

Size: 5" (13 cm)

Male: A small all brown bird with light brown marking on tail and wings. Often holds tail erect. Brown slightly curved bill.

Female: same as male

Juvenile: same as adult

Nest: cavity; female and male line just about any cavity; 2 broods per year

Eggs: 4-6; tan with brown markings

Incubation: 10-13 days; female and male incubate

Fledging: 12-15 days; female and male feed young

Migration: complete, to southern states and Mexico

Food: insects

Compare: Distinguished from the Carolina Wren (pg.76) by the lack of white stripe above eye. Look for upturned tail.

Stan's Notes: Prolific songsters, they sing from dawn to dusk during mating season. Easily attracted to nesting boxes. In spring, males choose several prospective nesting cavities and place a few small twigs in each. Female inspects each, chooses one, and finishes the nest building. She will completely fill nest cavity with uniformly small twigs then line a small depression at back of cavity with pine needles and grass. Often has trouble fitting long twigs through nest cavity hole, and tries many different directions and approaches until successful.

WINTER

PINE SISKIN
Carduelis pinus

Size: 5" (13 cm)

Male: Small brown finch with heavily streaked back, breast, and belly. Yellow on wing bars and at base of tail. Thin bill.

Female: same as male

Juvenile: similar to adult, with light yellow tinge throughout chest and chin

Nest: modified cup; female builds; 2 broods per year

Eggs: 3-4; greenish blue with brown markings

Incubation: 12-13 days; female incubates

Fledging: 14-15 days; female and male feed young

Migration: irruptive, moves around the state to find food

Food: seeds, insects, will come to seed feeders

Compare: Female American Goldfinch (pg. 248) lacks streaks and has white wing bars. Female House Finch (pg. 70) has streaked chest but lacks yellow wing bars. Female Purple Finch (pg. 84) has bold white eyebrow.

Stan's Notes: Usually considered a winter finch, this bird can be seen in flocks of up to 20 individuals and is often seen with Evening Grosbeaks (pg. 262). More commonly seen in the northern half of Illinois but can be found throughout the state in heavy invasion years; it is absent from Illinois in some winters. Will come to thistle feeders. Travels and breeds in small groups with nests often only a few feet apart. Males feed females during incubation. Juveniles lose yellow tint of chest and chin by late summer of first year.

CAROLINA WREN
Thryothorus ludovicianus

YEAR ROUND

Size: 5½" (14 cm)

Male: Warm rusty brown head and back with an orange yellow chest and belly. White throat and a prominent white eye stripe. Short stubby tail often cocked up.

Female: same as male

Juvenile: same as adults

Nest: cavity; female and male build, 2 broods per year, sometimes 3

Eggs: 4-6; white, sometimes pink or creamy, with brown markings

Incubation: 12-14 days; female incubates

Fledging: 12-14 days; female and male feed young

Migration: non-migrator

Food: insects, fruit, few seeds

Compare: Similar to the House Wren (pg. 72) but the Carolina Wren has the prominent white eyebrow. Look for the upturned tail.

Stan's Notes: Mates long term, remaining together throughout the year in permanent territories. Will sing throughout the year and the male is known to sing up to 40 different song types, singing one song repeatedly before switching to another. Females also sing, resulting in duets. Male often takes over feeding first brood of young while the female renests. Range expands northward in years with mild winters. Will nest in birdhouses or in the most unusual places, such as mailboxes, bumpers of cars, broken taillights, or just about any other cavity. Found in woodlands or brushy yards.

YEAR ROUND

SONG SPARROW
Melospiza melodia

Size: 5-6" (13-15 cm)

Male: Common brown sparrow with heavy dark streaks on chest coalescing into a central dark spot.

Female: same as male

Juvenile: similar to adult, finely streaked chest without central spot

Nest: cup; female builds; 2 broods per year

Eggs: 3-4; pale blue to green with reddish brown marks

Incubation: 12-14 days; female incubates

Fledging: 9-12 days; female and male feed young

Migration: complete, to southern states

Food: insects, seeds, rarely visits seed feeders

Compare: Similar to other brown sparrows, look for heavily streaked chest with central dark spot.

Stan's Notes: Many Song Sparrow sub-species or varieties, but central dark spot carries through each variant. While the female builds another nest for second brood, the male often takes over feeding the young. Returns to similar area each year, defending its small territory by singing from thick shrubs. Common host of Brown-headed Cowbird. Ground feeder, look for them to scratch simultaneously with both feet to expose seeds. Unlike many sparrow species, Song Sparrows rarely flock together.

male pg. 174

female

WINTER

DARK-EYED JUNCO
Junco hyemalis

Size: 5½" (14 cm)

Female: A round bird, with tan to brown chest, head and back. White belly, ivory to pink bill, and dark eye. Since the outermost tail feathers are white, the tail appears as a white "V" in flight.

Male: same as female, only slate gray to charcoal

Juvenile: similar to female, with streaked chest and head

Nest: cup; female and male build; 2 broods per year

Eggs: 3-5; white with reddish brown markings

Incubation: 12-13 days; female incubates

Fledging: 10-13 days; male and female feed young

Migration: complete, all across United States

Food: seeds, insects, will come to seed feeders

Compare: Rarely confused with other birds. Large flocks come to feed under bird feeders.

Stan's Notes: One of Illinois' most common winter birds. Usually seen on the ground in small flocks. Migrates from Canada to Illinois and beyond. Males tend to migrate farther south than females. Look for white outer tail feathers that flash in flight. Several species of Juncos have now been combined into one, simply called the Dark-eyed Junco. Most comfortable on the ground, Juncos "double-scratch" with both feet to expose seeds and insects. Consume many "weed" seeds. A flocking bird, it adheres to a rigid social hierarchy with dominant birds chasing less dominant birds.

female

male pg. 50

INDIGO BUNTING
Passerina cyanea

Size: 5½" (14 cm)

Female: Light brown finch-like bird with faint streaking on light tan chest. Wings have very faint blue cast with indistinct wing bars.

Male: vibrant blue finch-like bird, scattered dark markings on wings and tail

Juvenile: similar to female

Nest: cup; female builds; 2 broods per year

Eggs: 3-4; pale blue, unmarked

Incubation: 12-13 days; female incubates

Fledging: 10-11 days; female feeds young

Migration: complete, to Mexico, Central America and South America

Food: insects, seeds, fruit, will visit seed feeders

Compare: Similar to female finches. Female American Goldfinch (pg. 248) has white wing bars. Female Purple Finch (pg. 84) has heavily streaked chest and white eye lines. Female House Finch (pg. 70) also has heavily streaked chest.

Stan's Notes: A secretive bird, usually only the males are seen. Will come to feeders in spring before insects are plentiful. Mostly seen along woodland edges feeding on insects. Males often sing from tree tops to attract mates. A late migrant, with males returning before females and juveniles. Juveniles move to within a mile from birth site. Migrates at night in flocks of 5-10 birds.

male pg. 228

female

WINTER

PURPLE FINCH
Carpodacus purpureus

Size: 6" (15 cm)

Female: A plain brown bird with heavily streaked chest. Prominent white eye line.

Male: raspberry red head, cap, breast, back and rump, wings and tail brownish

Juvenile: same as female

Nest: cup; female and male build; 1 brood per year

Eggs: 4-5; greenish blue with brown markings

Incubation: 12-13 days; female incubates

Fledging: 13-14 days; female and male feed young

Migration: irruptive, moves around the state to find food

Food: seeds, insects, fruit, will come to seed feeders

Compare: Female House Finch (pg. 70) lacks white eyebrow. Pine Siskin (pg. 78) has yellow wing bars. Female American Goldfinch (pg. 248) has clear chest and white wing bars.

Stan's Notes: Usually only seen during winter when flocks of Purple Finches leave their northern homes and move around looking for food. Travels in flocks of up to 50. Comes to seed feeders along with House Finches, making it hard to tell them apart. A rich loud song and a distinctive "tic" note is made only in flight. Not a purple color, the name "purpureus" comes from the Latin meaning "crimson" or other reddish color.

side view

front view

WINTER

AMERICAN TREE SPARROW
Spizella arborea

Size: 6" (15 cm)

Male: A common brown sparrow with tan breast and rusty crown. Note single black spot in center of breast. Upper bill dark, lower bill yellow. Two white wing bars. Gray eyebrow.

Female: same as male

Juvenile: lacking rusty crown, has a streaked chest often obscuring the central dark spot

Nest: cup; female builds; 1 brood per year

Eggs: 3-5; green white with brown markings

Incubation: 12-13 days; only female incubates

Fledging: 8-10 days; female and male feed young

Migration: complete, throughout North America

Food: insects, seeds, occasionally comes to feeders

Compare: Looks similar to other sparrows so look closely for the single dark spot in the center of the breast. Shares a rusty crown with the Chipping Sparrow (pg. 68), but lacks the distinctive white and black eye line of the Chipping Sparrow. Song Sparrow (pg. 78) has a heavily streaked chest.

Stan's Notes: Seen mostly during spring and fall migration in small flocks of 2 to 200. They are a regular winter birdfeeder visitor throughout half of the state. Sometimes called the "winter chippy," since it looks similar to the Chipping Sparrow, a summer visitor. Nests in northern Canada.

EURASIAN TREE SPARROW
Passer montanus

YEAR ROUND

Size: 5-6" (13-15 cm)

Male: A brown head and back with a black throat and ear patch. Light brown to tan chest and belly.

Female: same as male

Juvenile: same as adults with duller throat and ear patch

Nest: cavity; female and male builds; 2-3 broods per year

Eggs: 4-6; white to gray with brown markings

Incubation: 13-14 days, female and male incubate

Fledging: 12-14 days, female and male feed young

Migration: non-migratory

Food: seeds and insects, will come to seed feeders

Compare: Nearly identical to the House Sparrow (pg. 90) but has a brown cap unlike the gray cap of the House Sparrow. Look for the black ear marking and brown cap to help identify.

Stan's Notes: Introduced from Germany in 1870 when 20 individual birds were released in St. Louis, Missouri. Since than the population has only spread a little into Missouri and Illinois with some recent sightings in Iowa. It is thought the more aggressive House Sparrow is the reason why they haven't spread further. Not really a sparrow but a type of Weaver bird. Often seen in parks and suburban yards and farmlands. Often goes unnoticed by the novice bird watcher. Often builds a nest of grass and small pieces of trash in natural cavities or nest boxes.

male

female

HOUSE SPARROW
Passer domesticus

YEAR ROUND

Size: 6" (15 cm)

Male: Medium sparrow-like bird with large black spot on chin extending down to chest. Brown back with white wing bar. Gray belly and crown.

Female: all light brown bird, lacking black throat patch and wing bar, slightly smaller

Juvenile: similar to female

Nest: domed cup nest, within cavity; female and male build; 2-3 broods per year

Eggs: 4-6; white, with brown markings

Incubation: 10-12 days; female incubates

Fledging: 14-17 days; female and male feed young

Migration: non-migrator, moves around to find food

Food: seeds, insect, fruit, comes to seed feeder

Compare: Nearly identical to the Eurasian Tree Sparrow (pg. 88) lacking the Eurasian's black mark on cheek. Look for the male House Sparrow's black bib to help identify. Female has clear chest and no marking on head (cap).

Stan's Notes: Introduced from Europe to Central Park, New York in 1850 and now found throughout North America. These birds are not really sparrows, but members of the Weaver Finch family characterized by large oversized domed nests. Constructs a nest containing scraps of plastic, paper, and whatever else is available. Aggressive bird that will kill the young of other birds in order to take over a cavity. Familiar city bird nearly always in flocks.

WHITE-THROATED SPARROW
Zonotrichia albicollis

Size: 6-7" (15-18 cm)

Male: A brown sparrow with gray tan chest and belly. Small yellow spot between eyes called lore. Distinctive white throat patch, crown has white or tan stripes alternating with black stripes.

Female: same as male

Juvenile: brown version of adult, eyebrow and throat gray with heavily streaked chest

Nest: cup; female builds; 1 brood per year

Eggs: 4-6; varies between greenish, bluish, and creamy white, with red brown markings

Incubation: 11-14 days; female incubates

Fledging: 10-12 days; female and male feed young

Migration: complete, to southern states and Mexico

Food: insects, fruit, seeds, will come to ground feeders

Compare: White-crowned Sparrow (pg. 94) has a black and white striped crown without yellow lores or white throat patch.

Stan's Notes: There are two color variations of White-throated Sparrows, called polymorphic; tan-striped and white-striped. Studies indicate the white-striped adults tend to mate with the tan-striped birds. No indication why. Nests are built on the ground under small trees in bogs and coniferous forest.

juvenile

MIGRATION
WINTER

WHITE-CROWNED SPARROW
Zonotrichia leucophrys

Size: 6½-7½" (16-19 cm)

Male: A brown sparrow with gray chest and a black-and-white striped crown. Small thin pink bill.

Female: same as male

Juvenile: similar to adults, with brown stripes on head instead of white

Nest: cup; female builds; 2 broods per year

Eggs: 3-5; varies between greenish, bluish, and whitish, with red brown markings

Incubation: 11-14 days; female incubates

Fledging: 8-12 days; male and female feed young

Migration: complete, to southern states and Mexico

Food: insects, seeds, berries, will come to ground feeders

Compare: White-throated Sparrow (pg. 92) has white or tan throat patch and yellow spot between eye and bill, with a blackish bill.

Stan's Notes: Doesn't nest in Illinois. Males take most of the responsibility of raising young while female starts a second brood. Only 9-12 days separate the broods. Feeds on the ground by scratching backwards with both feet at the same time. Usually seen in groups of up to 20 during spring and fall migration.

MIGRATION
WINTER

FOX SPARROW
Passerella iliaca

Size: 7" (18 cm)

Male: A plump, rusty-red sparrow. Heavily streaked rust-colored breast with a solid rust tail. Head and back are mottled with gray.

Female: same as male

Juvenile: same as adult

Nest: cup; female builds; 2 broods per year

Eggs: 2-4; pale green, with reddish markings

Incubation: 12-14 days; female incubates

Fledging: 10-11 days; female and male feed young

Migration: complete, to southern states

Food: insects, seeds, comes to feeders

Compare: Similar coloration as Brown Thrasher (pg. 118), but Fox Sparrow is smaller, plumper and has a smaller bill. Rusty color differentiates it from all other sparrows.

Stan's Notes: One of the largest sparrows, it is often only seen under seed feeders during spring and autumn migration. Scratches like a chicken with both feet at the same time to find seeds and insects. Nests on the ground in brush and forest edges in Canada. The name "sparrow" comes from the Anglo-Saxon word "spearwa," which means "flutterer," as applied to any small bird. "Fox" refers to the bird's rusty color.

male pg. 2

female

YEAR ROUND
SUMMER

EASTERN TOWHEE
Pipilo erythrophthalmus

Size: 7-8" (18-20 cm)

Female: A mostly light brown bird with rusty red brown sides and white belly. Long brown tail with white tip. Short, stout, pointed bill with rich red eye. White wing patches flash in flight.

Male: similar to female but is black not brown

Juvenile: light brown, heavily-streaked head, chest and belly; long dark tail with white tip

Nest: cup, female builds, 2 brood per year

Eggs: 3-4; creamy white with brown marking

Incubation: 12-13 days, female incubates

Fledging: 10-12 days, female and male feed young

Migration: complete, to southern states and South America

Food: insects, seeds, fruit; comes to ground feeder

Compare: Slightly smaller than the American Robin (pg. 188). Gray Catbird (pg. 186) lacks black hood and rusty sides. Common Grackle (pg. 10) lacks white belly and has a long thin bill. Female Rose-breasted Grosbeak (pg. 106) has striped chest and white eye mark.

Stan's Notes: Its uncommon name comes from its distinctive "tow-hee" call given by both sexes. Mostly known for its characteristic call that sounds like "drink your tea!" White eyed form in southern states. Seen hopping backward with both feet to rake up the leaf litter, called bilateral scratching, in search of insects and seeds. Female broods, but male does most of the feeding of young.

YEAR ROUND

CEDAR WAXWING
Bombycilla cedrorum

Size: 7½" (19 cm)

Male: A very sleek looking brown gray bird with a pointed crest on head, light yellow belly, and bandit-like black mask. The tip of its tail is bright yellow and the tips of its wings look as if they have been dipped in red wax.

Female: same as male

Juvenile: slightly smaller, lacking red wing tips, black mask, or sleek appearance, heavily streaked chest

Nest: cup; female and male build; 1 brood per year, occasionally 2

Eggs: 4-6; pale blue with brown markings

Incubation: 10-12 days; only female incubates

Fledging: 14-18 days; female and male feed young

Migration: partial migrator

Food: fruit, insects

Compare: Nearly identical to its larger, less common, cousin the Bohemian Waxwing.

Stan's Notes: Their name is derived from red wax-like wing tips and their preference for eating small blueberry-like cones of the cedar. Mostly seen in flocks, moving from area to area looking for berries. More often seen in winter only because naked branches reveal their presence. Spends most of its time at the tops of tall trees. In summer, before berries are abundant, they feed on insects. Listen for very high-pitched whistling sounds that the birds constantly make. Wanders in winter to find available food supplies.

male pg. 4

female

YEAR ROUND

BROWN-HEADED COWBIRD
Molothrus ater

Size: 7½" (19 cm)

Female: Dull brown gray bird without any obvious markings. Pointed, sharp gray bill.

Male: glossy black bird with chocolate brown head

Juvenile: similar to female only duller gray with streaked chest

Nest: no nest; lays eggs in nests of other birds

Eggs: 5-7; white with brown markings

Incubation: 10-13 days; host bird incubates eggs

Fledging: 10-11 days; host birds feed young

Migration: complete, to southern states

Food: insects, seeds, will come to seed feeders

Compare: In the blackbird family. The slightly larger female Red-winged Blackbird (pg. 112) has white eye line and streaked chest. European Starling (pg. 6) has speckles and long pointed yellow bill and short tail.

Stan's Notes: Of about 750 species of parasitic birds worldwide, this is the only parasitic bird in Illinois, laying all eggs in "host" birds' nests, leaving others to raise its young. Cowbirds are known to have laid eggs in nests of over 200 species of birds. Some birds reject cowbird eggs, but most raise them, even to the exclusion of their own young. Look for warblers and other birds feeding young birds twice their own size. At one time they followed bison to feed on the insects attracted to the animals.

HORNED LARK
Eremophila alpestris

Size: 7-8" (18-20 cm)

Male: A sleek tan to brown bird. Black necklace with yellow chin and black bill. Two tiny "horns" on top of head, which can be difficult to see. Black tail with white outer feathers noticeable in flight.

Female: same as male, only duller, horns less noticeable

Juvenile: lacks all black markings and yellow chin, doesn't form "horns" until second year

Nest: ground; female builds; 2 broods per year

Eggs: 3-4; gray with brown markings

Incubation: 11-12 days; female incubates

Fledging: 9-12 days; female and male feed young

Migration: complete, to Central and South America

Food: seeds, insects

Compare: Larger than House Sparrow (pg. 90). Look for a black mark on Horned Lark's face and neck.

Stan's Notes: The Lark name comes from the Middle English word "Laverock," or "a lark." Larks are birds of open ground. The only true Lark in North America. A very common bird in rural areas. Almost always seen in large flocks along country roads. Some pairs have up to 3 broods per year because they get such an early start. Females perform a fluttering distraction display if nest is disturbed. Females can renest about 7 days after brood fledges. Population increased over the past 100 years due to clearing land for farming.

105

female

male pg. 24

MIGRATION
SUMMER

ROSE-BREASTED GROSBEAK
Pheucticus ludovicianus

Size: 7-8" (18-20 cm)

Female: Plump, heavily streaked brown and white bird with obvious white eyebrow line. Wing linings are orange yellow.

Male: plump, black-and-white bird with large rose triangular patch on center of chest, wing linings are rosy red, large ivory bill

Juvenile: same as female

Nest: cup; female and male build; 1-2 broods per year

Eggs: 3-5; blue green with brown markings

Incubation: 13-14 days; female and male incubate

Fledging: 9-12 days; female and male feed young

Migration: complete, to Mexico, Central and South America

Food: insects, seeds, fruit, comes to seed feeders

Compare: Males are very distinctive with no look-alikes. Females look like large sparrows. Female is larger and has more distinctive eyebrow mark than female Purple Finch (pg. 84). Female House Finch (pg. 70) has no eyebrow mark.

Stan's Notes: Both males and females sing, but males sing much louder and clearer. Rich robin-like song. White wing patches flash when in flight. The name "Grosbeak" refers to its large bill used to crush seeds. The male's red breast patch varies in size and shape in each individual. Males arrive first in spring joined by females several days later. Late to arrive in spring and early to leave in autumn.

winter

breeding

SPOTTED SANDPIPER
Actitis macularia

SUMMER
MIGRATION

Size: 8" (20 cm)

Male: Olive brown back and white chest with black spots. White line over eye and short bill with long dull yellow legs. Lacks breast spots in fall and winter.

Female: same as male

Juvenile: similar to adult, lacking spots on chest and darker bill

Nest: ground; female and male build; 2 broods per year

Eggs: 3-4; brownish with brown markings

Incubation: 20-24 days; male incubates

Fledging: 17-21 days; male feeds young

Migration: complete, southern states and South America

Food: aquatic insects

Compare: Much smaller than the Greater Yellowlegs (pg. 132) and Lesser Yellowlegs (pg. 122). Look for Spotted Snadpiper's black spots extending from chest down to abdomen.

Stan's Notes: One of the more common Sandpipers, females mate with multiple males and lay eggs in up to 5 different nests. Males incubate and care for young. Constantly bobs tail while standing and walks as if delicately balanced. Flies with wings held in cup-like arc, never really lifted above a horizontal plane. Able to fly straight up out of the water. One of the few shorebirds that will actually dive underwater if pursued. When this bird is in its winter plumage, it lacks its spots.

male pg. 232

female

NORTHERN CARDINAL
Cardinalis cardinalis

YEAR ROUND

Size: 8-9" (20-23 cm)

Female: A buff brown bird with tinges of red on crest and wings, black mask and large red bill.

Male: red bird with black mask on face extending down to chin and throat, large red bill and crest on head

Juvenile: same as female, with blackish gray bill

Nest: cup; female builds; 2-3 broods per year

Eggs: 3-4; bluish white with brown markings

Incubation: 12-13 days; female and male incubate young

Fledging: 9-10 days; female and male feed young

Migration: non-migrator

Food: seeds, insects, fruit, will come to seed feeder

Compare: Female Cardinal appears similar to immature cardinal. Look for female's bright red bill.

Stan's Notes: A familiar backyard bird, look for male feeding female during courtship. Male feeds young of first brood by himself while female builds second nest. Their name comes from the Latin word "cardinalis" which means "important." Very territorial during spring, it will fight its own reflection in a window. Non-territorial in winter, they gather in small flocks of up to 20 birds. Both male and female sing, and can be heard any time of year. Listen for their "whata-cheer cheer cheer" territorial call in spring.

female

male pg. 8

RED-WINGED BLACKBIRD
Agelaius phoeniceus

Size: 8½" (22 cm)

Female: A heavily streaked brown bird with white eyebrow and pointed brown bill.

Male: jet black bird with red and yellow patch on upper wing, pointed black bill

Juvenile: same as female

Nest: cup; female builds; 2-3 broods per year

Eggs: 3-4; bluish green with brown markings

Incubation: 10-12 days; female incubates

Fledging: 11-14 days; female and male feed young

Migration: complete, to southern states, Mexico, and Central America

Food: insects, seeds, will come to seed feeder

Compare: Slightly larger than female Brown-headed Cowbird (pg. 102), which lacks white eyebrow and streaks on chest. Similar to female Rose-breasted Grosbeak (pg. 106), only thinner body and long pointed bill.

Stan's Notes: It is a sure sign of spring when the Red-winged Blackbirds return to the marsh. Flocks of up to 100,000 birds have been reported. Males return before females and defend territories. Will repeat call from top of cattail while showing off red and yellow wing bars called epaulets. Females choose mate. Nests are usually over shallow water in thick stand of cattails. One of the most widespread and numerous birds in Illinois. Feeds mostly on seeds in spring and fall, switching to insects during summer.

in flight

COMMON NIGHTHAWK
Chordeiles minor

SUMMER

Size: 9" (23 cm)

Male: A camouflaged brown and white bird with white chin and distinctive white bands across wings and tail only seen in flight.

Female: similar to male, but with tan chin and lacking white tail band

Juvenile: same as adult

Nest: no nest, lays eggs on ground, usually on rocks, or on roof top; 1 brood per year

Eggs: 2; cream with lavender markings

Incubation: 19-20 days; female and male incubate

Fledging: 20-21 days; female and male feed young

Migration: complete, to South America

Food: insects caught in air

Compare: Much larger than Chimney Swift (pg. 66). Look for obvious white wing bars of Nighthawk.

Stan's Notes: Usually only seen flying at dusk or after sunset, but not uncommon during the day. Prolific insect eater. One of the first birds to migrate each autumn. More common in the city than country. Prefers gravel rooftops for nesting. Very noisy birds, repeating a "peenting" call during flight. Alternates slow wing beats with bursts of quick wing beats. Males' distinctive springtime mating ritual is a steep diving flight terminated with a loud popping noise.

male

female

NORTHERN BOBWHITE
Colinus virginianus

Size: 10" (25 cm)

Male: A short stocky mostly brown bird with a short gray tail. A prominent white eye stripe and white throat. Reddish brown sides and belly often with black lines and dots.

Female: similar to male, but has a buffy brown eye stripe and throat

Juvenile: smaller and duller than adults

Nest: ground, female and male build; 1 brood per year

Eggs: 12-15; white to creamy, unmarked

Incubation: 23-24 days, female and male incubate

Fledging: 6-7 days, female and male feed young

Migration: non-migrator

Food: insects, seeds, fruit, comes to ground feeders offering corn and millet

Compare: Smaller and lacks long tail of the female Ring-necked Pheasant (pg. 152)

Stan's Notes: Moves around in small flocks of 20 birds called a covey. The covey often rest together at night, in a tight circle with tails together and heads facing outward to watch for predators. Both males and females perform a distraction display if the nest or young are threatened. Male gives a rising whistle "bob-white" heard mainly in spring and summer. Also gives a single "hoy" call year round. Prefers shrubs, orchards, hedgerows and pastures. Nest is nothing more than a depression in the ground lined with grass. Often pulls near by vegetation over the nest to help conceal it.

BROWN THRASHER
Toxostoma rufum

YEAR ROUND
SUMMER

Size: 11" (28 cm)

Male: A rusty red bird with long tail and heavily streaked chest and belly. Size and shape similar to Robin. Two white wing bars. Long curved bill and bright yellow eye.

Female: same as male

Juvenile: same as adult, eye color grayish

Nest: cup; female and male build; 2 broods per year

Eggs: 4-5; pale blue with brown markings

Incubation: 11-14 days; female and male incubate

Fledging: 10-13 days; female and male feed young

Migration: complete, to southern states

Food: insects, fruit

Compare: Similar in size and shape to the Gray Catbird (pg. 186), but Thrasher has a streaked chest and rusty color. Similar rusty color as the Fox Sparrow (pg. 96) but Thrasher is larger and thinner.

Stan's Notes: Prodigious songsters, they are often found in thick shrubs where they sing deliberate musical phrases, repeating each twice. The male has the largest documented song repertoire of all North American birds with over 1,100 song types. Often seen quickly flying in and out of thick or dense shrubs.

KILLDEER
Charadrius vociferus

YEAR ROUND
SUMMER

Size: 11" (28 cm)

Male: An upland shorebird with two black bands around neck like a necklace. Brown back and white belly. Bright reddish orange rump, visible in flight.

Female: same as male

Juvenile: similar to adults, but only one neck band

Nest: ground; male builds; 2 broods per year

Eggs: 3-5; tan with brown markings

Incubation: 24-28 days; male and female incubate

Fledging: 25 days; male and female lead young to food

Migration: complete, to southern states, Mexico, Central America

Food: insects

Compare: Only shorebird with two black neck bands.

Stan's Notes: Known for their broken-wing impression to draw intruders away from nest. Once clear of the nest the bird takes flight. Young look like yellow cotton balls on stilts. Able to follow parents and peck for insects soon after birth. Nests are only a slight depression in a gravel area, often very difficult to see. Has a very distinctive "kill-jer" call. Often found in vacant fields or along railroads. Technically classified as a shorebird, but doesn't live at the shore.

LESSER YELLOWLEGS
Tringa flavipes

MIGRATION

Size: 10-11" (25-28 cm)

Male: Typical sandpiper-type bird with brown back and wings, and lightly streaked white breast and belly. Thin straight black bill and long yellow legs.

Female: same as male

Juvenile: same as adult

Nest: ground; female builds; 1 brood per year

Eggs: 3-4; yellowish, with brown markings

Incubation: 22-23 days; male and female incubate

Fledging: 18-20 days; male and female lead young to food

Migration: complete, to South America

Food: insects

Compare: Nearly a carbon copy of Greater Yellowlegs (pg. 132), only smaller with shorter bill.

Stan's Notes: Usually seen in large flocks, they comb shorelines and mud flats looking for aquatic insects. They use their long straight bills to pluck insects and tiny fish from water. Very shy bird that quite often moves into the water prior to taking flight. Has a variety of "flight notes" that it gives when taking off. A member of the group of sandpipers called tattlers, all of which scream alarm calls when it takes flight. Most often seen in head down, tail up position walking along looking to snatch up something to eat. Nests on marshes in spruce forests of central Alaska and central Canada. Nest is a simple depression atop a mound of earth. Migrates later than Greater Yellowlegs in spring and earlier in fall.

123

male

female

AMERICAN KESTREL
Falco sparverius

Size: 10-12" (24-30 cm)

Male: Rusty brown back and tail. White chest with dark spots. Double black vertical lines on white face. Males have blue gray wings. Distinctive wide black band with white edge on tip of rusty tail.

Female: similar to male, slightly larger, but with rusty brown wings, and dark bands on tail

Juvenile: same as adult

Nest: cavity; doesn't build nest within; 1 brood per year

Eggs: 4-5; white with brown markings

Incubation: 29-31 days; male and female incubate

Fledging: 30-31 days; female and male feed young

Migration: complete, to southern states, Central America, small percentage non-migrator

Food: insects, small mammals and birds, reptiles

Compare: Similar to other falcons, such as less common Merlin and Peregrine. Look for the two vertical black stripes on face of Kestrel. No other small bird of prey has rusty colored back or tail.

Stan's Notes: Formerly called "Sparrow Hawk" due to its small size. Seen hovering near roads, before diving for prey. Adapts quickly to a wooden nesting box. Has pointed swept-back wings seen in flight. Perches nearly upright. Kestrels are the rare raptor in which the males and females have quite different markings. Watch for them to pump their tail up and down after landing on perch.

female

male

NORTHERN FLICKER
Colaptes auratus

YEAR ROUND

Size: 12" (30 cm)

Male: Brown and black woodpecker with a large white rump patch visible only when flying. Black necklace above a speckled breast. Red spot on nape of neck and black mustache.

Female: same as male, lacking black mustache

Juvenile: same as adult

Nest: cavity; female and male excavate; 1 brood per year

Eggs: 5-8; white, unmarked

Incubation: 11-14 days; female and male incubate

Fledging: 25-28 days; female and male feed young

Migration: complete, to southern states

Food: insects, especially ants

Compare: Yellow-bellied Sapsucker (pg. 26) is smaller and has red chin and forehead. Red-bellied Woodpecker (pg. 32) has a black-and-white zebra striped back and red patch on head, and lacks mustache. Flickers are the only brown backed woodpeckers in Illinois.

Stan's Notes: The Flicker is the only woodpecker to regularly feed on the ground, preferring ants and beetles. Produces an anti-acid saliva to neutralize the acidic defense of ants. Males usually select nest site, which takes up to 12 days to excavate. Flashes golden yellow under wings and tail in flight. Undulates deeply in flight while giving loud "wacka-wacka" call.

MOURNING DOVE
Zenaida macroura

Size: 12" (30 cm)

Male: Smooth, fawn colored dove with black spots on wings and tail. Single black spot behind and below eye. Pointed wedge-shaped tail with white edges. Gray patch on head, iridescent pink, green around neck.

Female: similar to male, lacks iridescent neck feathers

Juvenile: spotted and streaked, called a "squab"

Nest: platform; female and male build; 2 broods per year

Eggs: 2; white, unmarked

Incubation: 13-14 days; male and female incubate, male incubates during day, female at night

Fledging: 12-14 days; female and male feed young

Migration: partial migrator, moves around to find food, or to southern states

Food: seed, will come to seed feeders

Compare: Smaller than Rock Dove (pg. 194), lacking its wide range of color combinations.

Stan's Notes: They tend to mate for life, roughly 7-10 years. Builds a flimsy platform nest of twigs that often falls apart in a storm. Feeds on the ground. Look for head bobbing while walking. Parents feed the young a regurgitated liquid called crop-milk for the first few days of life. One of the few birds to drink without lifting head, same as Rock Dove. Name comes from its "mournful" cooing. Listen for characteristic whistling sound when they fly. This is caused by wind rushing through wing feathers.

PIED-BILLED GREBE
Podilymbus podiceps

Size: 13" (33 cm)

Male: Small brown water bird with a black chin and black ring around a thick, chicken-like ivory bill. Puffy white patch under the tail. Has an unmarked brown bill during winter.

Female: same as male

Juvenile: paler, with white spots, gray chest and belly, and gray bill

Nest: floating platform; female and male build, 1 brood per year

Eggs: 5-7; bluish white, unmarked

Incubation: 22-24 days; female and male incubate

Fledging: 22-24 days; female and male feed young

Migration: complete, to southern states, Mexico, and Central America

Food: aquatic insects, fish

Compare: The smallest brown water bird that dives underwater for long periods of time.

Stan's Notes: A very common water bird. Often seen diving for crayfish, aquatic insects, and fish. It slowly sinks like a submarine when disturbed. Formerly called "Hell-diver" because of the length of time it stays submerged. Can surface far away from where it went under. Builds a platform nest on a floating mat in water. Particularly sensitive to pollution. Adapted well to life on the water with short wings, lobed toes, and legs that are set close to rear of body. While swimming is easy, they are very awkward on land. The name "grebe" probably came from the Old English word "krib," meaning crest, a reference to the Great Crested Grebe found in Europe.

131

MIGRATION

GREATER YELLOWLEGS
Tringa melanoleuca

Size: 14" (35 cm)

Male: A tall bird with bulbous head and long thin bill slightly turned up. Gray streaking on chest and white belly. Long yellow legs.

Female: same as male

Juvenile: same as adult

Nest: ground; female builds; 1 brood per year

Eggs: 3-4; off white with brown markings

Incubation: 22-23 days; female and male incubate

Fledging: 18-20 days; male and female feed young

Migration: complete, to southern states and South America

Food: small fish, aquatic insects

Compare: Nearly identical to Lesser Yellowlegs (pg. 122), but 3" larger and longer upturned bill.

Stan's Notes: A common shorebird identified by slightly upturned bill and long yellow legs, often seen resting on one leg. Its long legs carry it through deep water. Nests on the ground near water on the northern tundra of Labrador and Newfoundland. Often seen feeding by rushing forward through the water, plowing its bill or swinging it from side to side, catching small insects or fish. A skittish bird, quick to give an alarm call causing flocks to take flight. Quite often moves into the water prior to taking flight. Has a variety of "flight" notes that it gives when taking off.

BLUE-WINGED TEAL
Anas discors

MIGRATION
SUMMER

Size: 15-16" (38-40 cm)

Male: Small, plain looking brown duck speckled with black. Gray head. Large white crescent-shaped mark at base of bill. Black tail with small white patch. Blue wing patch usually seen only in flight.

Female: duller version of male, lacking facial crescent mark and white tail markings

Juvenile: same as female

Nest: ground; female builds; 1 brood per year

Eggs: 8-11; creamy white

Incubation: 23-27 days; female incubates

Fledging: 35-44 days; female feeds young

Migration: complete, southern states, Central America

Food: aquatic plants, seeds, aquatic insects

Compare: Nearly half the size of female Mallard (pg. 150), which has a yellow bill. Female Blue-winged Teal similar to female Wood Duck (pg. 142) but lacks the Wood Duck's bright white eye ring and crest on head.

Stan's Notes: Males leave females near end of incubation. Females will perform distraction display to protect nest and young. Blue wing patch is called "speculum." Nest is built some distance from water. Planting crops and cultivating to pond's edge is causing a decline in population.

male pg. 34

female

MIGRATION
WINTER

LESSER SCAUP
Aythya affinis

Size: 16-17" (41-43 cm)

Female: An overall brown duck with a white patch at base of a light gray bill.

Male: white and gray, chest and head appear nearly black; in direct sun head appears purple with green highlights

Juvenile: same as female

Nest: ground; female builds; 1 brood per year

Eggs: 8-14; olive buff without markings

Incubation: 22-28 days, female incubates

Fledging: 45-50 days, female teaches young what to feed on

Migration: complete, to the southern states, northern South America, Central America

Food: aquatic plants and insects

Compare: Nearly identical to the slightly larger but much more uncommon Greater Scaup; male Blue-winged Teal (pg. 134) is smaller and has a bright white crescent shape patch near base of bill.

Stan's Notes: Probably one of the most common of all the diving ducks in Illinois. Often seen in large flocks numbering in the thousands on area lakes, ponds and sewage lagoons. Mostly seen during spring and fall migration. When seen in flight from below, they have a bold white stripe on the wings. Has an interesting baby sitting arrangement where the young form groups tended by 1-3 adult females.

soaring

BROAD-WINGED HAWK
Buteo platypterus

Size: 14-19" (35-48 cm)

Male: A small hawk no bigger than the American Crow, the Broad-wing has a brown back and rusty red "barring" on chest. Tail has 2 or 3 wide black-and-white bands. White under wings, with black "finger tips" when seen in flight.

Female: same as male

Juvenile: tail bands narrower and more numerous, brown streaked chest and belly

Nest: platform; female and male build but female finishes; 1 brood per year

Eggs: 2-3; off white with brown markings

Incubation: 28-32 days; female incubates, male feeds female while incubating

Fledging: 34-35 days; female and male feed young

Migration: complete, to Central and South America

Food: small mammals, small birds, large insects, snakes, frogs

Compare: Same size as Cooper's Hawk (pg. 198), but with wider, shorter tail. Slightly larger than Sharp-shinned Hawk (pg. 196). Note alternating white and black tail bands.

Stan's Notes: A very common hawk in Illinois. Often seen in large groups (kettles) migrating early in autumn. Massive migration provides a spectacular sight along the Great Lakes coastline. Spends most of its time hunting snakes, small birds, and frogs in dense woodlands. Short round wings propel it through dense woods.

female

male pg. 36

HOODED MERGANSER
Lophodytes cucullatus

MIGRATION
WINTER

Size:	16-19" (40-48 cm)
Female:	A long, thin, duck-like bird with long pointed bill, red head, ragged "hair" on back of head, gray body.
Male:	same size and shape as female, but black back, and rust sides, crest (hood) raises to reveal large white patch
Juvenile:	similar to female
Nest:	cavity; female lines former woodpecker hole; 1 brood per year
Eggs:	10-12; white, unmarked
Incubation:	32-33 days; female incubates
Fledging:	71 days; female feeds young
Migration:	complete, to gulf coast, Mexico
Food:	small fish, aquatic insects
Compare:	Smaller than female Common Merganser (pg. 234) lacking white chest.

Stan's Notes: Not as common as the Common Merganser, the male Hooded Merganser can voluntarily raise and lower the crest on its head to show off the large white patch. Females will "dump" eggs into other female Hooded Mergansers' nests resulting in 20-25 eggs in some nest. Mergansers have been known to share a nesting cavity with Goldeneyes and Wood Ducks sitting side by side.

141

male pg. 212

female

WOOD DUCK
Aix sponsa

YEAR ROUND
SUMMER

Size: 17-20" (43-51 cm)

Female: A small brown dabbling duck. Bright white eye ring and not so obvious crest. Blue patch on wing is often hidden.

Male: highly ornamented with a green head, red eye and crest, patterned with white and black, rusty chest and white belly

Juvenile: same as female

Nest: cavity; female lines former woodpecker cavity; 1 brood per year

Eggs: 10-15; creamy white, unmarked

Incubation: 28-36 days; female incubates

Fledging: 56-68 days; female teaches young to feed

Migration: complete, to southern states

Food: aquatic insects, plants, seeds

Compare: Smaller than the Northern Shoveler (pg. 146), and lacks the long wide bill. Smaller than female Mallard (pg. 150) which lacks the Wood Duck's white eye ring.

Stan's Notes: A common duck of quiet shallow backwater ponds. Nests in old woodpecker holes or nest boxes. Often seen flying deep within a forest or perched high up on branches of trees. Female enters nest cavity from full flight. Females will lay eggs in neighboring female nest, called "egg dumping," resulting in some clutches in excess of 20 eggs. Young remain in nest cavity only 24 hours after hatching, then jump from up to 30 feet to the ground or water to follow their mother. After that, they never return to the nest. Female takes flight with loud squealing call.

female

male pg. 40

WINTER

COMMON GOLDENEYE
Bucephala clangula

Size: 18½-20" (47-50 cm)

Female: A mostly gray duck with a white collar, a large dark brown head, and bright golden eyes.

Male: a mostly white duck with a black back, a large puffy green head, with a large white spot in front of each bright golden eye

Juvenile: same as female

Nest: cavity; female lines former woodpecker cavity; 1 brood per year

Eggs: 8-10; light green without markings

Incubation: 28-32 days; female incubates

Fledging: 56-59 days; female leads young to food

Migration: complete, to southern states

Food: aquatic plants, insects

Compare: Similar to, but larger than, the brown and white female Lesser Scaup (pg. 136).

Stan's Notes: Known for their loud whistling, which is produced by their wings in flight. In spring, males often attract females through elaborate displays, throwing their head backwards while uttering a single raspy note. Females will lay eggs in other Goldeneye nests, resulting in some mothers incubating up to 30 eggs. Received its common name from its obvious bright golden eyes.

male pg. 214

female

NORTHERN SHOVELER
Anas clypeata

Size: 20" (50 cm)

Female: A medium-sized brown duck speckled with black. Has an extraordinary large spoon-shaped bill almost always held pointed toward the water. Blue wing patch.

Male: same spoon-shaped bill, iridescent green head with rusty sides and a white breast

Juvenile: same as female

Nest: ground; female builds; 1 brood per year

Eggs: 9-12; olive, unmarked

Incubation: 22-25 days; female incubates

Fledging: 30-60 days; female leads young to food

Migration: complete, to southern states and Central America

Food: aquatic insects, plants

Compare: Similar to female Mallard (pg. 150). Check for spoon-shaped bill. Larger than female Wood Duck (pg. 142) lacking white eye ring.

Stan's Notes: Seen in small flocks of 5-10 swimming low in water with large bill always pointed towards water as if it's too heavy to lift. More commonly seen during spring migration. Feeds primarily by filtering tiny plants and insects from the water's surface with bill.

BARRED OWL
Strix varia

Size: 20-24" (50-60 cm)

Male: A chunky, brown and gray owl with dark horizontal "barring" on chest, and vertical streaking on belly. Large head with dark brown eyes.

Female: same as male only slightly larger

Juvenile: same as adult

Nest: cavity; no nesting material brought in; 1 brood per year

Eggs: 2-3; white, unmarked

Incubation: 28-33 days; female incubates

Fledging: 42-44 days; female and male feed young

Migration: non-migrator

Food: mammals, small birds

Compare: Lacks the "horns" of Great Horned Owl (pg. 158). It's our only owl with dark eyes. About twice the size of the tiny Eastern Screech-Owl (pg. 190).

Stan's Notes: A very common owl that can often be seen hunting during the day. Prefers dense woodlands with sparse undergrowth. Can be attracted with a simple nest box with a large opening attached to a tree. The young will stay with the parents for up to 4 months after fledging (leaving the nest). Often sounds like a dog barking just before giving an eight-hoot call which sounds like: "Who-cooks-for-you? Who-cooks-for-you?" Great Horned Owl sounds like: "Hoo-hoo-hoo-hoooo."

male pg. 218

female

YEAR ROUND

MALLARD
Anas platyrhynchos

Size: 27-28" (68-70 cm)

Female: All brown duck with orange and black bill and small blue and white wing mark, called speculum.

Male: large bulbous green head, white necklace and rust brown or chestnut chest, combination of gray and white on sides, yellow bill, legs, and feet

Juvenile: same as female but with yellow bill

Nest: ground; female builds; 1 brood per year

Eggs: 7-10; greenish to whitish, unmarked

Incubation: 26-30 days; female incubates

Fledging: 42-52 days; female leads young to food

Migration: complete, to southern states, small percentage non-migrator

Food: seeds, plants, aquatic insects, ground feeders offering corn

Compare: Female Northern Shoveler (pg. 146) is smaller and has a large spoon shaped bill. Female Wood Duck (pg. 142) is smaller and has white eye ring.

Stan's Notes: Familiar duck of lakes and ponds. Will return to place of birth. The name Mallard comes from the Latin "masculus," meaning "male," referring to the habit of males not taking part in raising ducklings. Both male and female have white tails and white underwings. Black central tail feathers of male curl upward.

male

female

YEAR ROUND

RING-NECKED PHEASANT
Phasianus colchicus

Size: 30-36" (75-90 cm), male, including tail
21-25" (53-63 cm), female, including tail

Male: Golden brown body with long tail. White ring around neck with purple, green, blue, and red head.

Female: smaller, less flamboyant all brown bird with long tail

Juvenile: similar to female with shorter tail

Nest: ground; female builds; 1 brood per year

Eggs: 8-10; olive brown, unmarked

Incubation: 23-25 days; female incubates

Fledging: 11-12 days; female leads young to food

Migration: non-migrator

Food: insects, seeds, fruit, will come to ground feeders

Compare: Nearly twice the size of the Northern Bobwhite (pg. 116). The Ring-necked Pheasant has a longer tail, and male is brightly colored.

Stan's Notes: Introduced from China in the late 1800s. Now common throughout the U.S. Like many game birds, their numbers vary greatly, making them common some years and scarce others. The common name (Ring-necked) refers to the thin white ring around the male's neck. The name "pheasant" comes from a Greek word, phaisianos, meaning "a bird of the River Phasis" which is now known as the River Rioni, located in Europe. Listen for male's "cackling" call to attract females.

153

male pg. 200

female

NORTHERN HARRIER
Circus cyaneus

Size: 24" (60 cm)

Female: dark brown back with brown streaked breast and belly, large white rump patch, narrow black bands across tail, tips of wings black

Male: A slim low-flying hawk. Silver gray with large white rump patch and white belly. Faint narrow bands across tail. Tips of wings black.

Juvenile: similar to female, with orange breast

Nest: platform; female and male build; 1 brood per year

Eggs: 4-8; bluish white, unmarked

Incubation: 31-32 days; female incubates

Fledging: 30-35 days; male and female feed young

Migration: complete, southern states, Central America

Food: mice, snakes

Compare: Slightly smaller than the Red-tailed Hawk (pg. 156). Look for bands on tail and white rump patch.

Stan's Notes: One of the easiest hawks to identify. Harriers glide just above ground following the contours of the land while searching for prey. Wings held just above the horizontal position, tilting back and forth in the wind, similar to Turkey Vultures. Formerly called Marsh Hawk due to its habit of hunting over marshes. Nests on the ground. At all ages, the Northern Harrier has distinctive "owl-like" face disks.

soaring

RED-TAILED HAWK
Buteo jamaicensis

YEAR ROUND

Size: 19-25" (48-63 cm); up to 4 foot wing span

Male: A large hawk with an amazing variety of colors from bird to bird, from chocolate brown to nearly all white. Often brown with white breast and distinctive brown belly band. Rust red tail usually only seen from above. Underside of wing white with small dark patch on leading edge near shoulder.

Female: same as male, often larger

Juvenile: similar to adult, lacking red tail with speckled chest

Nest: platform; male and female build; 1 brood per year

Eggs: 2-3; white, unmarked or occasionally marked with brown

Incubation: 30-35 days; female and male incubate

Fledging: 45-46 days; male and female feed young

Migration: partial migrant, to southern states, small percentage are non-migrator

Food: mice, birds, snakes, insects

Compare: Nearly twice the size of Sharp-shinned Hawk (pg. 196), Cooper's Hawk (pg. 198), and Broad-winged Hawk (pg. 138).

Stan's Notes: One of the most common hawks of open country and cities, often seen perched on freeway light posts. Look for it circling above open fields searching for prey. Will return to the same nest site each year. Doesn't develop red tail until second year.

GREAT HORNED OWL
Bubo virginianus

YEAR ROUND

Size: 20-25" (50-63 cm)

Male: Robust brown "horned" owl with bright yellow eyes, and V-shaped white bib.

Female: same as male, only slightly larger

Juvenile: similar to adults

Nest: no nest; takes over nest of crows, Great Blue Heron, and hawks, or uses partial cavities; 1 brood per year

Eggs: 2; white, unmarked

Incubation: 26-30 days; female incubates

Fledging: 30-35 days; male and female feed young

Migration: non-migrator

Food: small mammals, birds, snakes, insects

Compare: Barred Owl (pg. 148) has no horns and dark eyes. Over twice the size of the Eastern Screech-Owl (pg. 190).

Stan's Notes: Earliest nesting bird in Illinois, lays eggs in January and February. Has excellent hearing, able to hear a mouse moving under a foot of snow. "Ears" are actually tufts of feathers and have nothing to do with hearing. Not able to turn head all the way around. Wing feathers are ragged on the end resulting in a silent flight. Eyelids close from the top down, like humans. Fearless, it is one of the few animals that will kill skunks and porcupines. Because of this, they are sometimes called the "Flying Tiger."

YEAR ROUND

WILD TURKEY
Meleagris gallopavo

Size: 36-48" (90-120 cm)

Male: Large brown and bronze plump bird with striking blue and red bare head. Fan tail and long straight black beard in center of chest. Spurs on legs.

Female: thinner and less striking than male, lacking breast beard

Juvenile: same as female

Nest: ground; female builds; 1 brood per year

Eggs: 10-12; buff white with dull brown markings

Incubation: 27-28 days; female incubates

Fledging: 6-10 days; female leads young to food

Migration: non-migrator

Food: insects, seeds, fruit

Compare: This bird is distinctive and unlikely to be confused with others.

Stan's Notes: Eliminated from Illinois by the turn of the century due to market hunting and loss of habitat, they were reintroduced in the 1950-60s. Males hold "harems" of up to 20 females. Strong fliers, they can approach 60 mph. Able to fly straight up, then away. Eyesight three times better than humans. Their hearing is also excellent, able to hear competing males up to 1 mile away. Nearly became our national bird, but lost by one vote to the Bald Eagle. They roost in trees at night. The bird from which the domestic turkey was bred. Largest game bird in Illinois.

RUBY-CROWNED KINGLET
Regulus calendula

Size: 4" (10 cm)

Male: Small teardrop-shaped gray green bird with two white wing bars and a hidden ruby colored crown. White eye ring.

Female: same as male, lacks ruby crown

Juvenile: same as adult

Nest: pendulous; female builds; 1 brood per year

Eggs: 4-5; white with brown markings

Incubation: 11-12 days; female incubates

Fledging: 11-12 days; female and male feed young

Migration: complete, to southern states, Mexico and Central America

Food: insects, berries

Compare: Similar to Golden-crowned Kinglet (pg. 164), but crown is ruby-colored.

Stan's Notes: Most commonly seen during spring and autumn migration. It takes a quick eye to see the male's ruby crown. Look for small bird flitting around thick shrub low to the ground. The name "king-let" comes from the Anglo-Saxon word "cyning," or "king," referring to its ruby crown, and the diminutive suffix "let," meaning small. The second smallest bird in Illinois. Builds an unusual pendulous (sac-like) nest, intricately woven and suspended from a branch overlapped by leaves. Usually the nest is hung high in mature trees. It is decorated on the outside with colored lichens and mosses stuck together with spider webs.

WINTER

GOLDEN-CROWNED KINGLET
Regulus satrapa

Size: 4" (10 cm)

Male: A tiny plump gray green bird with a distinctive yellow and orange patch on crown, patch has black border. White eyebrow mark. Two white wing bars.

Female: same as male but has a yellow crown, lacking any orange

Juvenile: same as adults

Nest: pendulous; female builds; 1-2 broods a year

Eggs: 5-9; white or creamy with brown markings

Incubation: 14-15 days; female incubates

Fledging: 14-19 days; female and male feed young

Migration: complete to southern states, Mexico, Central America

Food: insects, fruit, tree sap

Compare: Similar to Ruby-crowned Kinglet (pg. 162) but Golden-crowned has an obvious crown. Smaller than the female American Goldfinch (pg. 248) which lacks any crown marking.

Stan's Notes: Common during winter in southern Illinois. Nests in northern conifer forests, including those in nearby central Wisconsin. Often seen in flocks that include chickadees, nuthatches, woodpeckers, Brown Creepers and Ruby-crowned Kinglets. Has a habit of flicking its wings when moving around. Unusual hanging nest is often made of moss, lichens and spider webs and lined with bark and feathers. Nest located 5-50 feet above ground. Can have so many eggs in its small nest that eggs are in two layers. Drinks tree sap and feeds by gleaning insects from trees. Can be very tame and approachable.

165

RED-BREASTED NUTHATCH
Sitta canadensis

WINTER

Size:	4½" (11 cm)
Male:	Small gray backed bird with black cap and prominent eye line. Rust red breast and belly.
Female:	gray cap, pale undersides
Juvenile:	same as female
Nest:	cavity; female builds; 1 brood per year
Eggs:	5-6; white with red brown markings
Incubation:	11-12 days; female incubates
Fledging:	14-20 days; female and male feed young
Migration:	irruptive, moves around the state to find food
Food:	insects, seeds, will come to seed and suet feeders
Compare:	Smaller than White-breasted Nuthatch (pg. 176) and has red breast instead of white.

Stan's Notes: Common during some winters and scarce during others, the Red-breasted Nuthatch behaves like the White-breasted Nuthatch, climbing "down" tree trunks head first. Visits seed feeders similar to chickadees, quickly grabbing one seed and flying off to crack it open. Will wedge a seed into a crevice and pound it open with several sharp blows. The name "nuthatch" comes from the old English moniker "nuthack," referring to the bird's habit of wedging a seed into a crevice and "hacking" it open. Look for them in mature conifers, frequently extracting seeds from cones. Doesn't excavate cavity as a chickadee might, rather takes over former woodpecker or chickadee cavity.

YEAR ROUND

BLACK-CAPPED CHICKADEE
Poecile atricapilla

Size: 5" (13 cm)

Male: Familiar gray bird with a black cap and throat patch. White chest and tan belly. Small white wing marks.

Female: same as male

Juvenile: same as adult

Nest: cavity; female and male build or excavate; 1 brood per year

Eggs: 5-7; white, fine brown markings

Incubation: 11-13 days; female and male incubate

Fledging: 14-18 days; female and male feed young

Migration: non-migrator

Food: insects, seeds, fruit, attracted to seed and suet feeders

Compare: Identical to Carolina Chickadee (pg. 170) except in song. Carolina's song is a higher and faster version of the Black-capped Chickadee's. Tufted Titmouse (pg. 178) has an erect crest on head.

Stan's Notes: A common backyard bird that can be attracted with a simple nest box. Makes nest mostly of green moss and lined with animal fur. Usually the first bird to find a new bird feeder. Can have different calls in various regions. Can be easily tamed and hand fed. Needs to feed everyday during winter, consequently seen foraging for food during even the worst winter storms.

CAROLINA CHICKADEE
Poecile carolinensis

Size: 5" (13 cm)

Male: A mostly gray bird with a black cap and chin. White face and chest with a tan belly. Darker gray tail.

Female: same as male

Juvenile: same as adult

Nest: cavity, female and male build or excavate; 1-2 broods per year

Eggs: 5-7; white with reddish brown markings

Incubation: 11-12 days, female and male incubates

Fledging: 13-17days, female and male feed young

Migration: non-migrator

Food: insects, seeds, fruit, comes to seed and suet feeders

Compare: Identical to the Black-capped Chickadee (pg. 168) except in song. Tufted Titmouse (pg. 178) has an erect crest on head, lacking the black cap and chin.

Stan's Notes: A common bird of southern Illinois. It will breed (hybridize) with the more northern Black-capped Chickadee where they meet. Can be attracted with a nest box with a 1¼" entrance hole. Females will give a loud snake-like hiss when disturbed on the nest. Often seen with other birds (mixed flock) during winter. A friendly bird that can be tamed and hand feed. Difficult to tell apart from the Black-capped Chickadee, best distinction is the song. Carolina's song is higher, faster version of the familiar "chik-a-dee-dee-dee-dee."

male

female

YELLOW-RUMPED WARBLER
Dendroica coronata

Size: 5-6" (13-15 cm)

Male: Slate gray bird with black mask and chest. Has yellow patch on head, flank, and rump. White chin and belly, two white wing bars.

Female: similar to male, duller in color, mostly brown and white with matching yellow patches

Juvenile: similar to female

Nest: cup; female builds; 2 broods per year

Eggs: 4-5; white with brown markings

Incubation: 12-13 days; female incubates

Fledging: 10-12 days; female and male feed young

Migration: complete, to southern states, Mexico, and Central America

Food: insects, berries, rarely comes to suet feeders

Compare: Similar to other warblers, look for the combination of yellow patches on head, flank, and rump to help identify this common warbler. Palm Warbler (pg. 254) has yellow chin and brown patch on head.

Stan's Notes: One of our most common warblers, seen in flocks of hundreds during spring and fall migration. Males molt to dull color similar to females each winter, retaining yellow patches. Formerly called the Myrtle Warbler. The only warbler to spend the winter in southern Illinois. Familiar call is a robust "chip."

female pg. 80

male

WINTER

DARK-EYED JUNCO
Junco hyemalis

Size: 5½" (14 cm)

Male: A round bird, with a slate gray to charcoal chest, head, and back. White belly, pink bill, and dark eye. Since the outermost tail feathers are white, the tail appears as a white "V" in flight.

Female: same as male, only tan to brown color

Juvenile: similar to female, with streaked chest and head

Nest: cup; female and male build; 2 broods per year

Eggs: 3-5; white with reddish brown markings

Incubation: 12-13 days; female incubates

Fledging: 10-13 days; male and female feed young

Migration: complete, all across United States

Food: seeds, insects, will come to seed feeders

Compare: Rarely confused with other birds. Large flocks come to feed under bird feeders.

Stan's Notes: One of Illinois' most common winter birds. Usually seen on the ground in small flocks. Migrates from Canada to Illinois and beyond. Males tend to migrate farther south than females. Look for white outer tail feathers that flash in flight. Several species of Juncos have now been combined into one, simply called the Dark-eyed Junco. Most comfortable on the ground, Juncos "double-scratch" with both feet to expose seeds and insects. Consume many "weed" seeds. A flocking bird, it adheres to a rigid social hierarchy with dominant birds chasing less dominant birds.

WHITE-BREASTED NUTHATCH
Sitta carolinensis

YEAR ROUND

Size: 5-6" (13-15 cm)

Male: Slate gray bird with white belly and black cap and neck. Long thin bill slightly upturned. Chestnut colored under tail.

Female: similar to male, gray cap and neck

Juvenile: same as adult

Nest: cavity; female and male build; 1 brood per year

Eggs: 5-7; white with brown markings

Incubation: 11-12 days; female incubates

Fledging: 13-14 days; female and male feed young

Migration: non-migrator

Food: insects, seeds, will come to seed and suet feeders

Compare: Red-breasted Nuthatch (pg. 166) is smaller and has rusty belly and distinctive black eye line.

Stan's Notes: The Nuthatchs' habit of hopping headfirst down tree trunks helps them see insects and eggs that birds climbing up the trunk might miss. The name "nuthatch" comes from the old English moniker "nuthack," referring to the bird's habit of wedging a seed into a crevice and "hacking" it open. Often seen in mixed flocks of Chickadees, Brown Creepers, and Downy Woodpeckers. Mated pairs remain together all year, defending their small territories. Listen for characteristic spring time call, "whi, whi, whi, whi," given during February and March. One of 17 worldwide nuthatch species. Incredible climbing agility comes from an extra long hind toe claw or nail, nearly twice the size of front toe claws.

TUFTED TITMOUSE
Baeolophus bicolor

Size: 6" (15 cm)

Male: Slate gray bird with a white chest and belly. Flanks washed in rusty brown. Gray legs and dark eyes. Pointed crest.

Female: same as male

Juvenile: same as adult

Nest: cavity, takes over old woodpecker hole; female builds; 2 broods per year

Eggs: 5-7; white with brown markings

Incubation: 13-14 days; only female incubates

Fledging: 15-18 days; female and male feed young

Migration: non-migrator

Food: insects, seeds, fruit, comes to seed and suet feeders

Compare: Closely related to Black-capped Chickadee (pg. 168) and Carolina Chickadee (pg. 170), but slightly larger. Chickadee lacks crest of the Tufted Titmouse. Similar in size and color to White-breasted Nuthatch (pg. 176), but Nuthatch doesn't have a crest.

Stan's Notes: The prefix "tit" comes from a Scandinavian word meaning "little." The suffix "mouse" is derived from the Old English word "mase" which means bird. Simply translated, it is "a small bird." Notorious for pulling hair from sleeping dogs, cats, and squirrels to line their nest. Attracted with nest boxes. Usually seen only one or two at a time. Male feeds female during courtship and nesting.

EASTERN PHOEBE
Sayornis phoebe

Size: 7" (18 cm)

Male: Gray green bird with dark wings, light olive green belly, and a thin, dark bill.

Female: same as male

Juvenile: same as adult

Nest: cup; female builds; 2 broods per year

Eggs: 4-5; white, unmarked

Incubation: 15-16 days; female incubates

Fledging: 15-16 days; male and female feed young

Migration: complete, to southern states, Mexico

Food: insects

Compare: Like most olive green birds, it is hard to distinguish any identifying markings. Eastern Phoebe lacks any white eye ring. Easier to identify by well enunciated song, "phoe-be," or characteristic of "hawking" for insects.

Stan's Notes: A sparrow-sized bird often seen on the end of a dead branch. It sits waiting for a passing insect, flies out to catch it, and then returns to the same branch, a process called "hawking." Will build nest under the eaves of a house, under a bridge, or in culverts, made of mud, grass, and moss. The nest is lined with hair and feathers. Name derived from its characteristic song repeated over and over from the top of dead branch "phoe-be." Phoebe has a habit of "pumping" and "spreading" its tail when perched.

EASTERN KINGBIRD
Tyrannus tyrannus

SUMMER

Size: 8" (22 cm)

Male: Mostly black gray bird with white belly and chin. Black head and tail with a distinctive white band across the end of tail. Has a concealed red crown that is rarely seen.

Female: same as male

Juvenile: same as adult

Nest: cup; male and female build; 1 brood per year

Eggs: 3-4; white with brown markings

Incubation: 16-18 days; female incubates

Fledging: 16-18 days; female and male feed young

Migration: complete, to Central America, South America

Food: insects, fruit

Compare: Rarely confused with other birds. Medium-sized bird, smaller than the American Robin (pg. 188). Look for the white band along the end of the tail to identify.

Stan's Notes: A common bird of open fields and prairies. Perceived as having an attitude, acting unafraid of other birds, and chasing larger birds. Bold behavior gives them their common name of "king." Perches on tall branches watching for insects. After flying out to catch them, returns to the same perch, a technique called "hawking." Males and females return to mating grounds and will defend a territory together.

SUMMER

GREAT CRESTED FLYCATCHER
Myiarchus crinitus

Size: 8" (20 cm)

Male: Gray head and back with a prominent crest on head. Gray throat with bright yellow belly extending down under reddish brown tail. Lower bill is yellow at base.

Female: same as male

Juvenile: same as adults

Nest: cavity; female and male build, 1 brood a year

Number of Eggs: 4-6

Eggs: white or buff with brown markings

Incubation: 13-15 days; female incubates

Fledging: 14-21 days; female and male feed young

Migration: complete to Mexico and Central America

Food: insects, fruit

Compare: The Eastern Kingbird (pg. 182) has a white band across the tail. Similar to Eastern Phoebe (pg. 180) but the Great Crested Flycatcher has obvious crest and yellow belly. The only "crested" flycatcher in eastern U.S.

Stan's Notes: A common bird of just about any wooded area, it lives high up in the trees rarely coming to the ground. Often heard before seen. Feeds by "gleaning" insects from the leaves of trees. Nests in old woodpecker holes but can be attracted to a nest box with an entrance hole of 1½ - 2½" placed high in a tree. Often stuffs nest with a collection of fur, feathers, string and snakeskins. Breeds throughout Illinois.

GRAY CATBIRD
Dumetella carolinensis

SUMMER

Size: 9" (23 cm)

Male: A handsome slate gray bird with a black crown. Long thin black bill. Often seen with tail lifted exposing chestnut colored patch under tail.

Female: same as male

Juvenile: same as adult

Nest: cup; female and male build; 2 broods per year

Eggs: 4-6; blue green, unmarked

Incubation: 12-13 days; female incubates

Fledging: 10-11 days; female and male feed young

Migration: complete, to southern states

Food: insects, fruit

Compare: Larger than Eastern Phoebe (pg. 180), it lacks the Phoebe's olive belly. Similar size to Eastern Kingbird (pg. 182), but it lacks the Kingbird's white belly and white tail band.

Stan's Notes: A secretive bird that the Chippewa Indians named "the bird that cries with grief" due to its raspy call. Its call sounds like a house cat's mewing, hence its common name. It often mimics other birds, rarely repeating the same phrases. It will only nest in thick shrubs and is more often heard than seen. It quickly flies back into the shrubs when approached. If a cowbird introduces an egg into a catbird nest, the catbird will quickly break then eject it.

male

female

AMERICAN ROBIN
Turdus migratorius

YEAR ROUND

Size: 9-11" (23-28 cm)

Male: Familiar gray bird with rusty red chest, nearly black head and tail, and black streaks on white chin. White eye ring.

Female: similar to male, but has a gray head and duller chest

Juvenile: similar to female, but has speckled chest and brown back

Nest: cup; female builds with help from male; 2 broods per year

Eggs: 4-7; pale blue, unmarked

Incubation: 12-14 days; female incubates

Fledging: 14-16 days; female and male feed young

Migration: complete, to southern states and Central America, small percentage will not migrate

Food: insects, fruit, berries, worms

Compare: Familiar bird to all.

Stan's Notes: Most people don't realize how easy it is to tell the difference between the male and female Robin. Look for the male's dark, nearly black head compared to the female's gray head. Robins are not listening for worms when they cock their heads to one side or the other. They are looking with eyes that are placed far back on the sides of their heads. Small percentage will not migrate but spend the winter in low swampy areas where they search for left-over berries and insect eggs. Some of these non-migrators will die before spring.

EASTERN SCREECH-OWL
Otus asio

YEAR ROUND

Size: 9" (22 cm)

Male: A small eared owl that occurs in one of two permanent color phases. Birds are either mottled with gray and white or they are red brown with white. Bright yellow eyes.

Female: same as male

Juvenile: lighter gray than adults, may lack the ear tufts

Nest: cavity, old woodpecker cavity; 1 brood per year

Eggs: 4-5; white, unmarked

Incubation: 25-26 dayas; female incubates; male feeds female on nest

Fledging: 26-27 days; male and female feed young

Migration: non-migrator

Food: large insects, small mammals, birds, snakes

Compare: The only small owl with ear tufts. Can be gray or rust colored.

Stan's Notes: A common owl active at dusk and at night. Excellent hearing and eyesight. Seldom gives a "screech" call, more commonly gives a tremulous, descending whiny trill that sounds like it came from the sound track of a scarry movie. Will nest in wooden nest box. Often seen sunning themselves at nestbox holes during winter. Male and female may roost together at night, and are thought to mate for life. Different color phases are called "morphs." Gray morph more common than red.

displaying

YEAR ROUND
MIGRATION
SUMMER

NORTHERN MOCKINGBIRD
Mimus polyglottos

Size: 10" (25 cm)

Male: Silvery gray head and back with light gray chest and belly. White wing patches, seen in flight or during display. Tail black with white outer tail feathers. Black bill.

Female: same as male.

Juvenile: overall dull gray with a heavily-streaked chest, gray bill

Nest: cup; female and male build, 2 broods per year, sometimes more

Eggs: 3-5; blue green with brown markings

Incubation: 12-13 days; female incubates

Fledging: 11-13 days; female and male feed young

Migration: partial migrator in northern states

Food: insects, fruit

Compare: Similar to Brown Thrasher (pg. 118) but thrasher is rusty red with spotted chest. Gray Catbird (pg. 186) is slate gray lacking the Mockingbird's white wing patches. Look for the Mockingbird to spread it wings to "flash" its white wing patches and "wag" its tail from side to side.

Stan's Notes: Very animated, both male and female perform elaborate mating dance by facing each other, heads and tails erect. They run towards each other flashing white wing patches then retreat to nearby cover. Known to imitate other birds, called "vocal mimicry," hence its common name. Young males often sing at night.

ROCK DOVE
Columba livia

YEAR ROUND

Size: 13" (33 cm)

Male: No set color pattern, gray to white with patches of iridescent greens and blues, usually with a light rump patch.

Female: same as male

Juvenile: same as adult

Nest: platform; female builds; 3-4 broods per year

Eggs: 1-2; white, unmarked

Incubation: 18-20 days; female and male incubate

Fledging: 25-26 days; female and male feed young

Migration: non-migrator

Food: seeds

Compare: Larger than light-brown-colored Mourning Dove (pg. 128).

Stan's Notes: Also known as the Domestic Pigeon, it was introduced to North America from Europe by early settlers. Most common around cities and barnyards, where it scratches for seeds. The wide color variation comes from years of selective breeding while in captivity. Parents feed young a regurgitated liquid called crop-milk the first few days of life. One of the few birds that can drink without tilting head back. Nests under bridges, on buildings, balconies, barns, and sheds. Once poisoned as a "nuisance city bird," many cities have Peregrine Falcons that feed on Rock Doves, keeping their numbers in check.

soaring

SHARP-SHINNED HAWK
Accipiter striatus

WINTER

Size: 10-14" (25-35 cm)

Male: A small woodland hawk with gray brown back and head. Rusty red breast with long tail with several dark tail bands, widest band at end of squared-off tail. Red eye.

Female: same as male, only larger

Juvenile: same size as adult, with brown back and heavily streaked breast, yellow eye

Nest: platform; female builds; 1 brood per year

Eggs: 4-5; white with brown markings

Incubation: 32-35 days; female incubates

Fledging: 24-27 days; female and male feed young

Migration: complete, southern states, Mexico, and Central America

Food: birds, small mammals

Compare: Nearly identical to Cooper's Hawk (pg. 198), only smaller. Look for squared end of tail on Sharp-shinned compared to round end of Cooper's.

Stan's Notes: A common hawk of backyards and woodlands, they are often seen swooping in on birds visiting feeders. Short rounded wings and long tail allow this hawk to navigate through thick stands of trees in pursuit of prey. Called "sharp-shinned" because of sharp keel on the leading edge of its "shin," although it is actually below rather than above the bird's ankle on the tarsus bone of foot. The tarsus in most birds is round. Rarely seen in winter. In flight, head doesn't protrude as far as the head of the Cooper's Hawk.

soaring

COOPER'S HAWK
Accipiter cooperii

YEAR ROUND

Size: 14-20" (35-50 cm)

Male: A medium hawk with short wings and a long rounded tail with several black bands. Rusty chest and dark wing tips. Slate gray back with a bright yellow spot at base of gray bill called a cere. Red eye.

Female: similar to male, only slightly larger

Juvenile: brown back with brown streaks on chest, yellow eye

Nest: platform; male and female build; 1 brood per year

Eggs: 2-4; greenish with brown markings

Incubation: 32-36 days; female and male incubate

Fledging: 28-32 days; male and female feed young

Migration: non-migrator to partial migrator, to southern states and Mexico

Food: small birds, mammals

Compare: Nearly identical to the Sharp-shinned Hawk (pg. 196), only larger, darker gray, and with a rounded-off tail.

Stan's Notes: A common hawk of the woodlands. In flight, look for its large head, short wings and proportionately long tail. Short stubby wings help it maneuver between trees while pursuing small birds. Will come to feeders hunting for unaware birds. Flies with long glides followed by a few quick flaps. Known to "ambush" their prey, they fly into heavy brush or even run the on ground in pursuit. Nestlings have gray eyes that become bright yellow at one year and later dark red. Can be seen during winter.

male

female pg. 154

NORTHERN HARRIER
Circus cyaneus

MIGRATION
WINTER

Size: 24" (60 cm)

Male: A slim low-flying hawk. Silver gray with large white rump patch and white belly. Faint narrow bands across tail. Tips of wings black.

Female: dark brown back with brown streaked breast and belly, large white rump patch, narrow black bands across tail, tips of wings black

Juvenile: similar to female, with orange breast

Nest: platform; female and male build; 1 brood per year

Eggs: 4-8; bluish white, unmarked

Incubation: 31-32 days; female incubates

Fledging: 30-35 days; male and female feed young

Migration: complete, southern states, Central America

Food: mice, snakes

Compare: Slightly smaller than the Red-tailed Hawk (pg. 156). Look for bands on tail and white rump patch.

Stan's Notes: One of the easiest hawks to identify. Harriers glide just above ground following the contours of the land while searching for prey. Wings held just above the horizontal position, tilting back and forth in the wind, similar to Turkey Vultures. Formerly called Marsh Hawk due to its habit of hunting over marshes. Nests on the ground. At all ages, the Northern Harrier has distinctive "owl-like" face disks.

CANADA GOOSE
Branta canadensis

Size: 25-43" (63-108 cm)

Male: Large gray goose with black neck and head with a white chin or cheek strap.

Female: same as male

Juvenile: same as adult

Nest: ground; female builds; 1 brood per year

Eggs: 5-10; white, unmarked

Incubation: 25-30 days; female incubates

Fledging: 42-55 days

Migration: non-migrator to partial migrator, to southern states

Food: aquatic plants, insects, seeds

Compare: A very common bird, hardly ever confused with any other bird.

Stan's Notes: Once not very common, they have adapted to our changed environment very well. Adults will mate for many years, and will only start to breed in their third year. Males often act as sentinels, standing on the edge of the group and bobbing their heads up and down, becoming very aggressive to anyone who approaches. Will hiss as if to display displeasure. Adults molt primary flight feathers while raising young, rendering family groups flightless at the same time. Several sub-species vary geographically around the United States. Generally they are paler in color in eastern and darker in western groups. Their size decreases northward, with the smallest subspecies found on the Arctic tundra. Introduced into several parts of the state, they are now breeding in Illinois and are common year-round residents.

MIGRATION
SUMMER

SANDHILL CRANE
Grus canadensis

Size: 40-48" (100-120 cm); up to 6-7 foot wing span

Male: Elegant gray birds with long legs and neck. Wings and body often stained rusty brown. Scarlet red cap on head with red eye.

Female: same as male

Juvenile: dull brown without red cap, yellow eye

Nest: platform nest on the ground; female and male build; 1 brood per year

Eggs: 2; olive with brown markings

Incubation: 28-32 days; female and male incubate

Fledging: 65 days; female and male feed young

Migration: complete, southern states and Mexico

Food: insects, fruit, worms, plants, amphibians

Compare: Similar size to the Great Blue Heron (pg. 206), but Sandhill has a shorter bill and a red patch on head. Great Blue Heron flies with neck held in S-shape compared to the Sandhill's straight neck.

Stan's Notes: Usually seen in large undisturbed fields near water. Often heard before seen, they have a very distinctive rattling call. Plumage often appears rust brown because of staining from mud during preening. Characteristic flight with up stroke quicker than down. For their spectacular mating dance, the performers face each other, bow, and jump into the air while uttering a loud cackling sound, and flapping wings.

GREAT BLUE HERON
Ardea herodias

Size: 42-52" (105-130 cm)

Male: Tall gray heron with black eyebrow extending into several long plumes off back of head. Long yellow bill. Feathers at base of neck drop down in a kind of necklace.

Female: same as male

Juvenile: same as adult but more brown than gray with a black crown and no plumes.

Nest: platform; male and female build; 1 brood per year

Eggs: 3-5; blue green, unmarked

Incubation: 27-28 days; female and male incubate

Fledging: 56-60 days; male and female feed young

Migration: complete, to southern states, Central and South America

Food: small fish, frogs, insects, snakes

Compare: Same size as Sandhill Crane (pg. 204), but lacks Sandhill's red crown. Sandhill flies with neck held straight compared to the Great Blue Heron's S-shaped neck.

Stan's Notes: One of the most common herons, it often barks like a dog when startled. Seen stalking small fish in shallow water. Will strike at mice, squirrels, and just about anything else it might come across. Flies holding neck in "S" shape, with its long legs trailing straight out behind. Wings held in cupped fashion during flight. Nests in colonies of up to 100 birds. Nests in tree tops near or over open water.

RUBY-THROATED HUMMINGBIRD
Archilochus colubris

SUMMER
MIGRATION

Size: 3-3½" (8-9 cm)

Male: Tiny iridescent green bird with black throat patch that reflects bright ruby red in sunlight.

Female: same as male, lacking throat patch

Juvenile: same as female

Nest: cup; female builds; 1-2 broods per year

Eggs: 2; white, unmarked

Incubation: 12-14 days; female incubates

Fledging: 14-18 days; female feeds young

Migration: complete, southern states, Mexico and Central America

Food: nectar, insects

Compare: No other bird this small. Sphinx Moth hovers at flowers like hummingbird, but has clear wings and a mouth part that looks like a straw that coils up when not at flower. Moves much slower than hummingbird and can be approached.

Stan's Notes: Wings create a "humming" noise, flapping 50-60 times per second or faster during chasing flights. Able to hover, fly up and down, and is the only bird to fly backwards. Constructs nest with plant material and spider webs, gluing pieces of lichen on outside of nest for decoration. Attracted to tubular red flowers. Weights only 2-3 grams, it takes about 5 average-sized hummingbirds to equal the weight of a single chickadee. Heart beats at an incredible 1,260 times a minute and breathes 250 times a minute. Does not "sing" but will chatter or buzz to communicate.

SUMMER

GREEN HERON
Butorides virescens

Size: 16-22" (40-55 cm)

Male: A short stocky heron with a blue-green back, rusty red neck and chest. Dark green crest. Short legs, normally yellow, but turn bright orange during the breeding season.

Female: same as male

Juvenile: similar to adult with blue-gray back and white streaked chest and neck

Nest: platform, female and male build, 2 broods per year

Eggs: 2-4; light green, unmarked

Incubation: 21-25 days, female and male incubates

Fledging: 35-36 days, female and male feed young

Migration: complete, to South America

Food: fish, insects, aquatic plants

Compare: Much smaller than Great Blue Heron (pg 206). Look for a small heron stalking along lakeshore with dark green back.

Stan's Notes: Often gives an explosive rasping "skyew" when startled. Sometimes it looks like it doesn't have a neck because it holds its head close to its body. Hunts for fish and aquatic insects by waiting along a shore or wades stealthily. Has been known to place an object like an insect on the water surface to attract fish to catch. Has a crest that it raises when excited.

male

female pg. 142

WOOD DUCK
Aix sponsa

YEAR ROUND
SUMMER

Size: 17-20" (43-51 cm)

Male: A small highly ornamented dabbling duck with a green head and crest, red eye, patterned with white and black. Rusty chest and white belly.

Female: brown, similar size and shape to male, has bright white eye ring and not so obvious crest, blue patch on wing often hidden

Juvenile: same as female

Nest: cavity; female lines former woodpecker cavity; 1 brood per year

Eggs: 10-15; creamy white, unmarked

Incubation: 28-36 days; female incubates

Fledging: 56-68 days; female teaches young to feed

Migration: complete, to southern states

Food: aquatic insects, plants, seeds

Compare: Smaller than the Northern Shoveler (pg. 214), and lacks the Shoveler's long wide bill.

Stan's Notes: A common duck of quiet shallow backwater ponds. Nests in old woodpecker holes or nest boxes. Often seen flying deep within a forest or perched high up on branches of trees. Female enters nest cavity from full flight. Females will lay eggs in neighboring female nest, called "egg dumping," resulting in some clutches in excess of 20 eggs. Young remain in nest cavity only 24 hours after hatching, then jump from up to 30 feet to the ground or water to follow their mother. After that, they never return to the nest. Nearly extinct around 1900 due to over hunting, but doing well now.

male

female pg. 146

NORTHERN SHOVELER
Anas clypeata

Size: 20" (50 cm)

Male: A medium-sized duck. Has an extraordinarily large spoon-shaped bill almost always held pointed toward the water. Iridescent green head with rusty sides and a white breast.

Female: same spoon-shaped bill, with brown and black over all and blue wing patch

Juvenile: same as female

Nest: ground; female builds; 1 brood per year

Eggs: 9-12; olive, unmarked

Incubation: 22-25 days; female incubates

Fledging: 30-60 days; female leads young to food

Migration: complete, to southern states and Central America

Food: aquatic insects, plants

Compare: Male is similar to Mallard (pg. 218), but Shoveler has large characteristic spoon-shaped bill. Much larger than male Wood Duck (pg. 212) and lacks Wood Duck's crest on head.

Stan's Notes: Seen in small flocks of 5-10 swimming low in water with large bill always pointed towards water as if it's too heavy to lift. More commonly seen during spring migration. Feeds primarily by filtering tiny plants and insects from the water's surface with bill.

female pg. 234

male

COMMON MERGANSER
Mergus merganser

WINTER

Size: 27" (68 cm)

Male: A long, thin, duck-like bird with a long pointed bill, green head, black back, and white sides, chest, and neck.

Female: same size and shape as male, but with rust red head, ragged "hair" on crest, gray body, and white chest

Juvenile: same as female

Nest: cavity; female lines former woodpecker cavity; 1 brood per year

Eggs: 9-11; ivory without markings

Incubation: 28-33 days; female incubates

Fledging: 70-80 days; female feeds young

Migration: complete, to southern states, Central America, Mexico

Food: fish, aquatic insects

Compare: Male Hooded Merganser (pg. 36) has white patch on head and rust red sides.

Stan's Notes: Mergansers are shallow water divers that feed on small fish in no more than 10 or 15 feet of water. More commonly seen along rivers than lakes. Their bills have a fine serrated-like edge to help catch slippery fish. Females often lay eggs in other Merganser nests, called "egg dumping," resulting in broods of up to 15 young per mother. The male leaves the female as soon as she starts to incubate eggs. Young that lose their mother will be accepted by other Merganser mothers with young.

female pg. 150

male

YEAR ROUND

MALLARD
Anas platyrhynchos

Size: 27-28" (68-70 cm)

Male: Large bulbous green head, white necklace and rust brown or chestnut chest. Combination of gray and white on sides. Yellow bill, legs, and feet.

Female: all brown duck with orange and black bill and small blue and white wing mark, called speculum

Juvenile: same as female but with yellow bill

Nest: ground; female builds; 1 brood per year

Eggs: 7-10; greenish to whitish, unmarked

Incubation: 26-30 days; female incubates

Fledging: 42-52 days; female leads young to food

Migration: complete, to southern states, small percentage non-migrator

Food: seeds, plants, aquatic insects, ground feeders offering corn

Compare: Male Northern Shoveler (pg. 214) has white chest with rust on sides and dark spoon-shaped bill.

Stan's Notes: Familiar duck of lakes and ponds. Will return to place of birth. The name Mallard comes from the Latin "masculus," meaning "male," referring to the habit of males not taking part in raising ducklings. Both male and female have white tails and white underwings. Black central tail feathers of male curl upward.

male

female pg. 246

MIGRATION
SUMMER

AMERICAN REDSTART
Setophaga ruticilla

Size: 5" (13 cm)

Male: A small striking black bird with contrasting patches of orange on sides, wings and tail. White belly.

Female: olive brown, with yellow patches instead of the male's orange, white belly

Juvenile: same as female, immature males tinged orange for first year

Nest: cup; female builds; 1 brood per year

Eggs: 3-5; off white with brown markings

Incubation: 12 days; only female incubates

Fledging: 9 days; female and male feed young

Migration: complete, to Mexico, Central and South America

Food: insects, seeds, berries rarely

Compare: Red-winged Blackbird (pg. 8) and Baltimore Oriole (pg. 222) are considerably larger, at roughly eight inches. Only small black and orange bird flitting around tops of trees.

Stan's Notes: A common and widespread warbler in Illinois. Prefers large unbroken tracts of forests. Appears to be hyperactive when feeding, hovering and darting back and forth to glean insects from leaves. Look for flashing black and orange color high in the trees. They often droop wings and fan tail just before launching out to catch an insect.

male

female pg. 258

SUMMER

BALTIMORE ORIOLE
Icterus galbula

Size: 7-8" (18-20 cm)

Male: Bright, flaming orange bird with black head and black extending down nape of neck onto back. Black wings with white and orange wing bars. Orange tail with black streaks.

Female: pale yellow bird with gray brown wings, white wing bars, gray bill, and dark eye

Juvenile: same as female

Nest: pendulous; female builds; 1 brood per year

Eggs: 4-5; bluish with brown markings

Incubation: 12-14 days; female incubates

Fledging: 12-14 days; female and male feed young

Migration: complete, to Mexico, Central and South America

Food: insects, fruit, nectar, will come to orange halves and nectar feeders

Compare: American Redstart (pg. 222) is several inches smaller and has more black than orange.

Stan's Notes: Fantastic songsters, you are likely to hear this bird before seeing it. Easily attracted to a feeder offering grape jelly, orange halves, or sugar water (nectar). Parents bring young to feeders. They build their sock-like nest at the outermost branches of tall trees. They often return to the same area year after year. Some of the last birds to arrive in spring (May) and first to leave in fall (September). They sit in the tops of the trees feeding on caterpillars.

female pg. 260

male

ORCHARD ORIOLE
Icterus spurius

MIGRATION
SUMMER

Size: 7-8" (18-20 cm)

Male: Dull orange bird with black head, and black extending down the back; black chin wings and tail. A single white wing bar. Long thin black bill with a small gray mark on lower mandible (jaw).

Female: olive green back with a dull yellow belly, two white wing bars on dark gray wings

Juvenile: similar as female

Nest: pendulous; female builds; 1 brood per year

Eggs: 3-5; pale blue to white with brown markings

Incubation: 11-12 days, female and male incubates

Fledging: 11-14 days, female and male feed young

Migration: complete, to Central Mexico, and Northern South America

Food: insects, fruit, comes to fruit/nectar feeders

Compare: Similar to the Baltimore Oriole (pg. 222) but Orchard Oriole has a much darker orange body.

Stan's Notes: Prefers open woods and orchards hence its common name. They eat insects until wild fruits start to ripen. One of the last birds to arrive in spring and one of the first to leave each fall, spending only about 3 to 4 months in Illinois. More common in southern Illinois. Usually nests alone but sometimes in small colonies. Parents bring young to jelly and orange half feeders shortly after fledging. Many people mistakenly think the orioles have left during summer, but in fact they are concentrating on finding insects to feed their young.

female pg. 70

male

HOUSE FINCH
Carpodacus mexicanus

YEAR ROUND

Size: 5" (13 cm)

Male: Orange red face, chest, and rump, with a dark marking behind eye. Brown wings streaked with white. White belly with brown streaks. Brown cap.

Female: brown with heavily streaked white chest

Juvenile: similar to female

Nest: cup, sometimes in cavities; female builds; 2 broods per year

Eggs: 4-5; pale blue, lightly marked

Incubation: 12-14 days; female incubates

Fledging: 15-19 days; female and male feed young

Migration: non-migrator to partial migrator, moves around to find food

Food: seeds, fruit, leaf buds, will come to seed feeder

Compare: Very similar to Purple Finch (pg. 228), lacking the Purple Finch's red cap. Look for the streaked chest and belly and darker face and head marking.

Stan's Notes: A relatively new bird to Illinois, it was originally introduced to Long Island, New York in the 1940s from western America. A very social bird, it visits feeders in small flocks. Seems to prefer nesting in hanging flower baskets. Incubating female is fed by male. Loud and cheerful warbling song.

female pg. 84

male

WINTER

PURPLE FINCH
Carpodacus purpureus

Size: 6" (15 cm)

Male: Raspberry red head, cap, breast, back and rump. Wings and tail brownish.

Female: heavily streaked brown and white with large white eye line

Juvenile: same as female

Nest: cup; female and male build; 1 brood per year

Eggs: 4-5; greenish blue with brown markings

Incubation: 12-13 days; female incubates

Fledging: 13-14 days; female and male feed young

Migration: irruptive, moves around the state to find food

Food: seeds, insects, fruit, will come to seed feeders

Compare: Redder than the orange red House Finch (pg. 226), with a clear (no streaking) red breast. House Finch has brown cap compared to Purple Finch's red cap.

Stan's Notes: Usually only seen during winter when flocks of Purple Finches leave their northern homes and move around looking for food. Travels in flocks of up to 50. Comes to seed feeders along with House Finches, making it hard to tell them apart. A rich loud song and a distinctive "tic" note is made only in flight. Not a purple color, the name "purpureus" comes from the Latin meaning "crimson" or other reddish color.

female
pg. 256

male

SCARLET TANAGER
Piranga olivacea

SUMMER

Size: 7" (18 cm)

Male: Bright scarlet red bird with jet black wings and tail. Ivory bill and dark eye.

Female: drab greenish yellow with olive wings and tail, ivory bill with dark eye

Juvenile: same as female

Nest: platform; female builds; 1 brood per year

Eggs: 4-5; blue green with brown markings

Incubation: 13-14 days; female incubates

Fledging: 9-11 days; female and male feed young

Migration: complete, to Central and South America

Food: insects, fruit

Compare: Northern Cardinal (pg. 232) has black mask and red bill, but lacks the black wings of the Scarlet Tanager.

Stan's Notes: Male sheds (molts) its bright red plumage in fall and winter, appearing more like the female. Prefers mature unbroken woodlands where it hunts for insects high in the tops of trees. Requires a minimum of 4 acres for nesting. Prefers 8 acres. A tropical-looking bird, they arrive late in spring and leave early in autumn. Scarlet Tanager is one of some 240 tanager species in the world. Nearly all brightly colored and live in the tropics. The name "tanager" comes from South American Tupi Indian word meaning any small, brightly colored bird.

female pg. 110

male

YEAR ROUND

NORTHERN CARDINAL
Cardinalis cardinalis

Size: 8-9" (20-23 cm)

Male: All red bird with black mask on face extending down to chin and throat. Large red bill and crest on head.

Female: buff brown with tinges of red on crest and wings, same black mask and red bill

Juvenile: same as female, with blackish gray bill

Nest: cup; female builds; 2-3 broods per year

Eggs: 3-4; bluish white with brown markings

Incubation: 12-13 days; female and male incubate young

Fledging: 9-10 days; female and male feed young

Migration: non-migrator

Food: seeds, insects, fruit, will come to seed feeder

Compare: Scarlet Tanager (pg. 230) has black wings and tail.

Stan's Notes: A familiar backyard bird, look for male feeding female during courtship. Male feeds young of first brood by himself while female builds second nest. Their name comes from the Latin word "cardinalis" which means "important." Very territorial during spring, it will fight its own reflection in a window. Non-territorial in winter, they gather in small flocks of up to 20 birds. Both male and females sing, and can be heard any time of year.

male pg. 216

female

COMMON MERGANSER
Mergus merganser

WINTER

Size: 27" (68 cm)

Female: A long, thin duck-like bird with rust red head, ragged "hair" on back of head, gray body, and white chest.

Male: same size and shape as female with a long pointed bill, green head, black back, and white sides, chest, and neck

Juvenile: same as female

Nest: cavity; female lines former woodpecker cavity; 1 brood per year

Eggs: 9-11; ivory without markings

Incubation: 28-33 days; female incubates

Fledging: 70-80 days; female feeds young

Migration: complete, to southern states, Central America, Mexico

Food: fish, aquatic insects

Compare: Female Hooded Merganser (pg. 140) has similar shape but is much smaller with a brown head.

Stan's Notes: Mergansers are shallow water divers that feed on small fish in no more than 10 or 15 feet of water. More commonly seen along rivers than lakes. Their bills have a fine serrated-like edge to help catch slippery fish. Females often lay eggs in other Merganser nests, called "egg dumping," resulting in broods of up to 15 young per mother. The male leaves the female as soon as she starts to incubate eggs. Young that lose their mother will be accepted by other mothers with young.

YEAR ROUND
MIGRATION

RING-BILLED GULL
Larus delawarensis

Size: 19" (48 cm)

Male: White bird with gray wings, black wing tips spotted with white, and white tail seen in flight. Yellow bill with a black "ring" near tip, Yellowish legs and feet.

Female: same as male

Juvenile: mostly gray version of adult, with a dark band at end of tail

Nest: ground; female and male build; 1 brood per year

Eggs: 2-4; off white with brown markings

Incubation: 20-21 days; female and male incubate

Fledging: 20-40 days; female and male feed young

Migration: complete, to southern states, Mexico

Food: insects, fish, scavenges

Compare: Similar to Herring Gull (pg. 238) which has an orange mark on tip of lower bill. Herring Gull has pink legs and feet and lacks Ring-billed's black ring.

Stan's Notes: This is the common gull of garbage dumps and parking lots. They are expanding their range and remain further north longer due to successful scavenging in cities. They acquire a new and different plumage in each of the first three falls and don't attain adult plumage until third year. They attain ring on bill after first winter.

YEAR ROUND
MIGRATION
WINTER

HERRING GULL
Larus argentatus

Size: 23-26" (58-65 cm)

Male: Common "sea gull" of large lakes. A snow-white bird with slate gray wings and black wing tips with tiny white spots. Yellow bill with red spot near tip of lower mandible. Pinkish legs.

Female: same as male

Juvenile: uniformly mottled brown to gray, black bill

Nest: ground, female and male build, 1 brood per year

Eggs: 2-3; olive with brown markings

Incubation: 24-28 days, female and male incubates

Fledging: 35-36 days, female and male feed young

Migration: complete, to coasts that remain unfrozen in North America

Food: fish, insects, clams, eggs, baby birds

Compare: Larger than Ring-billed Gull (pg. 236) which has a black ring around bill and lacks orange dot on lower mandible. Ring-billed Gull has yellow legs compared to Herring Gulls pinkish legs.

Stan's Notes: An opportunistic bird, scavenging for food from dumpsters but will also take other birds eggs and young right from nest. Often drops clams and other shellfish from heights to break shells and to get the soft interior. Nest in colonies, returning to same site year after year. Lines ground nest with grasses and seaweed. Adults molt to a dirty gray appears in winter, looking similar to juveniles. Takes about four years for juveniles to obtain adult plumage.

blue morph

white morph

SNOW GOOSE
Chen caerulescens

MIGRATION
WINTER

Size: 25-38" (63-95 cm)

Male: A mostly white goose with varying patches of black and brown. Black wing tips and pink bill and legs.

Female: same as male

Juvenile: overall dull gray with dark bill

Nest: ground; female builds; 1 brood per year

Eggs: 3-5; white, unmarked

Incubation: 23-25 days; female incubates

Fledging: 45-49 days; female and male teach young what to eat

Migration: complete, to southern states and Mexico

Food: aquatic insects and plants

Compare: Mute Swan (pg. 244) is twice the size of Snow Goose. Look for black wing tips of Snow Goose. Smaller than Canada Goose (pg. 202), lacking black neck and white chin strap.

Stan's Notes: Has a thick serrated bill to pull up plants. There are two color types, called phases or morphs. The gray phase often called "blue" with a white head, pink bill and legs, and gray chest and back. The other is pure white with black wing tip. Breeds in large colonies on the tundra of northern Canada. Females don't breed until 2-3 years old. Older females produce more eggs and are more successful than younger. Seen by the thousands during migration.

GREAT EGRET
Ardea alba

MIGRATION
SUMMER

Size: 38" (95 cm)

Male: Tall, thin, all white, elegant bird with long pointed yellow bill. Black, stilt-like legs and feet.

Female: same as male

Juvenile: same as adult

Nest: platform; male and female build; 1 brood per year

Eggs: 2-3; light blue, unmarked

Incubation: 23-26 days; female and male incubate

Fledging: 43-49 days; female and male feed young

Migration: complete, to southern states, Mexico and Central America

Food: fish, aquatic insects, frogs, crayfish

Compare: Larger than Snowy Egret, which also has a black bill but has yellow feet. Similar in size and shape to Great Blue Heron (pg. 206).

Stan's Notes: A tall, stately bird, the Great Egret slowly stalks shallow wetlands looking for small fish to spear with its long sharp bill. Nests in colonies of up to 100 birds. Now protected, they were hunted to near extinction for their long white plumage. The name "egret" came from the French word, "aigrette," which means "ornamental tufts of plumes." The plumes are grown near the tail during breeding season.

MUTE SWAN
Cygnus olor

WINTER
SUMMER

Size: 60" (152 cm)

Male: All white with prominent black knob at base of a large orange bill. Holds neck in an S-shape with bill pointed towards the surface of the water.

Female: same as male

Juvenile: brown to gray; gray bill with black base lacks the prominent knob

Nest: ground, female and male build; 1 brood per year

Eggs: 4-8; light gray lacking any markings

Incubation: 35-40 days, female incubates with help from male

Fledging: 115-150 days, female and male feed young

Migration: partial-migrator, moves to areas with open water during winter

Food: aquatic insects and plants

Compare: Very similar to Trumpeter and Tundra Swans but has an orange bill with a prominent knob near the face. Nearly twice the size of the Snow Goose (pg. 240), and lacking black wing tips.

Stan's Notes: An introduced species usually found in parks, zoos and golf courses is now found in the wild. Often swims with wings held arched over its back. Its neck always held in an S-shape. Trumpeter and Tundra Swans lack these features. Can be a very aggressive bird giving a loud hiss when disturbed or threatened.

male pg. 220

female

AMERICAN REDSTART
Setophaga ruticilla

Size: 5" (13 cm)

Female: Olive brown, with yellow patches on wings, sides, and tail. White belly.

Male: small striking black bird with contrasting patches of orange on wings, sides, and tail, white belly

Juvenile: same as female, immature males tinged orange for first year

Nest: cup; female builds; 1 brood per year

Eggs: 3-5; off white with brown markings

Incubation: 12 days; only female incubates

Fledging: 9 days; female and male feed young

Migration: complete, to Mexico, Central and South America

Food: insects, seeds, berries rarely

Compare: Similar to female Yellow-rumped Warbler (pg. 172) lacking the Warbler's yellow rump.

Stan's Notes: A common and widespread warbler in Illinois. Prefers large unbroken tracts of forests. Appears to be hyperactive when feeding, hovering and darting back and forth to glean insects from leaves. Look for flashing black and orange color high in the trees. They often droop wings and fan tail just before launching out to catch an insect.

male

female

AMERICAN GOLDFINCH
Carduelis tristis

Size: 5" (13 cm)

Male: A perky yellow bird with a black patch on forehead. Black tail with conspicuous white rump. Black wings with white wing bars. No marking on the chest. Dramatic change in color during winter, similar to female.

Female: dull olive yellow without a black crown, brown black wings and white rump

Juvenile: same as female

Nest: cup; female builds; 1 brood per year

Eggs: 4-6; pale blue, unmarked

Incubation: 10-12 days; female incubates

Fledging: 11-17 days; female and male feed young

Migration: partial migrator, moves around North America in flocks of up to 20

Food: seeds, insects, will come to seed feeders

Compare: Confused with other winter birds. Pine Siskin (pg. 74) has streaked chest and belly and "yellow" wing bars. Female Purple Finch (pg. 84) has heavily streaked chest and white line above eye. Larger female House Finch (pg. 70) has a streaked chest and belly.

Stan's Notes: Often called "Wild Canary." Feeder bird that enjoys Nyger Thistle. Late summer nesting, uses silky down from wild thistle for nest. Appears roller coaster-like in flight. Listen for them to twitter during flight. Almost always in small flocks. Moves only far enough south to find food. Small percentage stay all winter.

SUMMER

COMMON YELLOWTHROAT
Geothlypis trichas

Size: 5" (13 cm)

Male: An olive brown bird with bright yellow throat and breast, and white belly. Distinctive black mask outlined in white. Long thin pointed black bill.

Female: same as male, only lacking black mask

Juvenile: same as female

Nest: cup; female builds; 2 broods per year

Eggs: 3-5; white with brown markings

Incubation: 11-12 days; female incubates

Fledging: 10-11 days; female and male feed young

Migration: complete, to southern states, Central America

Food: insects

Compare: Found in similar habitat as American Goldfinch (pg. 248), but lacks its black crown and wing bars. Yellow Warbler (pg. 252) has fine orange streaks on chest and lacks black mask. Yellow-rumped Warbler (pg. 172) only has spots of yellow, compared to Yellowthroat's yellow breast.

Stan's Notes: A common warbler of open fields and marshes. A frequent Cowbird host. Young remain dependent upon parents longer than most warblers. It has a cheerful, well-known song, "witchity-witchity-witchity-witchity." Males perform a curious courtship display, bouncing in and out of tall grass while uttering an unusual song.

SUMMER

YELLOW WARBLER
Dendroica petechia

Size: 5" (13 cm)

Male: Yellow warbler with orange streaks on the chest and belly. Long pointed dark bill.

Female: same as male, lacking orange streaking

Juvenile: similar to adult, only much duller

Nest: cup; female builds; 1 brood per year

Eggs: 4-5; white with brown markings

Incubation: 11-12 days; female incubates

Fledging: 10-12 days; female and male feed young

Migration: complete, to southern states, Mexico, Central and South America

Food: insects

Compare: Look for orange streaking on chest of male. Male American Goldfinch (pg. 248) has black wings and cap. Female Yellow Warbler is similar to female American Goldfinch (pg. 248), lacking its white wing bars.

Stan's Notes: A common warbler of gardens and shrubby areas not far from water. Males often seen higher up in trees than females. Females are less conspicuous. Starts to migrate south in July and is complete in August. Migrates at night in mixed flocks of other warblers. Rests and feeds during the day.

PALM WARBLER
Dendroica palmarum

MIGRATION

Size: 5½" (14 cm)

Male: A warbler with distinctive yellow eyebrow and throat, belly and undertail. An obvious chestnut colored crown. Thin chestnut colored streaks on sides of breast. Dark line running through a dark eye.

Female: same as male

Juvenile: same as adult but duller and brown

Nest: cup, female builds; 1-2 broods per year

Eggs: 4-5; white with brown markings

Incubation: 11- 12 days, female incubates

Fledging: 12- 13 days, female and male feed young

Migration: complete, to Florida, Central America, West Indies

Food: insects, fruit

Compare: Similar size as the Yellow Warbler (pg. 252) Look for the Chestnut colored crown and yellow eyebrow. Yellow-rumped Warbler (pg. 172) lacks yellow throat and belly.

Stan's Notes: One of the most common and abundant warblers. Usually the second warbler to be seen during spring migration. The most common being the Yellow-rumped Warbler. Nests at the edge of northern spruce bogs. Often seen in backyard woodlands during spring and fall migration. Look for it to wag or bob its tail while gleaning bugs from the leaves and flowers of trees. One of the few warblers that feeds on the ground. Hops rather than walks. Recognizes cowbird eggs and will destroy the eggs by burying them with a new nest built right over the top of the old nest.

255

female

male pg. 230

SCARLET TANAGER
Piranga olivacea

Size: 7" (18 cm)

Female: Drab greenish yellow with olive wings and tail. Ivory bill with dark eye. Whitish wing linings.

Male: bright scarlet red bird with jet black wings and tail, ivory bill and dark eye

Juvenile: same as female

Nest: platform; female builds; 1 brood per year

Eggs: 4-5; blue green with brown markings

Incubation: 13-14 days; female incubates

Fledging: 9-11 days; female and male feed young

Migration: complete, to Central and South America

Food: insects, fruit

Compare: Female Northern Cardinal (pg. 110) has black mask and red bill, but lacks the dark wings of the female Scarlet Tanager. Larger than female American Goldfinch (pg. 248) and lacks Goldfinch's white wing bars. Female Baltimore Oriole (pg. 258) has gray bill and white wing bars.

Stan's Notes: Male sheds (molts) its bright red plumage in fall and winter, appearing more like the female. Prefers mature unbroken woodlands where it hunts for insects high in the tops of trees. Requires a minimum of 4 acres for nesting. Prefers 8 acres. A tropical-looking bird, they arrive late in spring and leave early in autumn. Scarlet Tanager is one of some 240 tanager species in the world. Nearly all brightly colored and live in the tropics. The name "tanager" comes from South American Tupi Indian word meaning any small, brightly colored bird.

male pg. 222

female

BALTIMORE ORIOLE
Icterus galbula

SUMMER

Size: 7-8" (18-20 cm)

Female: Pale yellow bird with gray brown wings, white wing bars. Gray bill and dark eye.

Male: bright, flaming orange bird with black head and black extending down nape of neck onto back, black wings with white and orange wing bars, orange tail with black streaks, gray bill and dark eye

Juvenile: same as female

Nest: pendulous; female builds; 1 brood per year

Eggs: 4-5; bluish with brown markings

Incubation: 12-14 days; female incubates

Fledging: 12-14 days; female and male feed young

Migration: complete, to Mexico, Central and South America

Food: insects, fruit, nectar, will come to orange halves and nectar feeders

Compare: The female Oriole, often confused with female Scarlet Tanager (pg. 256) which has olive colored wings.

Stan's Notes: Fantastic songsters, you are likely to hear this bird before seeing it. Easily attracted to a feeder offering grape jelly, orange halves, or sugar water (nectar). Parents bring young to feeders. They build their sock-like nest at the outermost branches of tall trees. They often return to the same area year after year. Some of the last birds to arrive in spring (May) and first to leave in fall (September). They sit in the tops of the trees feeding on caterpillars.

fe°

ORCHARD ORIOLE
Icterus spurius

MIGRATION
SUMMER

Size: 7-8" (18-20 cm)

Female: A olive green bird with a dull yellow belly, two white wing bars on dark gray wings. Long thin black bill with a small gray mark on lower mandible (jaw).

Male: dull orange with a black head, chin, upper back, wings and tail; single white wing bar

Juvenile: same as female

Nest: pendulous; female builds; 1 brood per year

Eggs: 3-5; pale blue to white with brown markings

Incubation: 11-12 days, female and male incubates

Fledging: 11-14 days, female and male feed young

Migration: complete to Central Mexico and Northern South America

Food: insects, fruit, comes to fruit/nectar feeders

Compare: Similar to female Baltimore Oriole (pg. 258) which is smaller with a brighter yellow belly. Smaller female Scarlet Tanager (pg. 256) has a large yellow bill and olive colored head.

Stan's Notes: Prefers open woods and orchards hence its common name. They eat insects until wild fruits start to ripen. One of the last birds to arrive in spring and one of the first to leave each fall, spending only about 3 to 4 months in Illinois. More common in southern Illinois. Usually nests alone but sometimes in small colonies. Parents bring young to jelly and orange half feeders shortly after fledging. Many people mistakenly think the orioles have left during summer, but in fact they are concentrating on finding insects to feed their young.

male

female

EVENING GROSBEAK
Coccothraustes vespertinus

MIGRATION
WINTER

Size: 8" (20 cm)

Male: A striking bird with a stocky body, large ivory to greenish bill, bright yellow eyebrows, a dirty yellow head, black-and-white wings and tail, and yellow rump and belly.

Female: similar to male, with softer colors, and gray head and throat

Juvenile: same as female, brown bill

Nest: cup; female builds; 1 brood per year

Eggs: 3-4; blue with brown markings

Incubation: 12-14 days; female incubates

Fledging: 13-14 days; female and male feed young

Migration: irruptive, seasonal movement brings birds to Illinois during winter

Food: seeds, insects, fruit, comes to seed feeders

Compare: Larger than its close relative the American Goldfinch (pg. 248). Look for the dark head with bright yellow eyebrow and extra large bill.

Stan's Notes: One of the largest finches. Has characteristic undulating "finch" flight. Has unusually large bill for cracking seeds, its main source of food. Often seen along gravel roads eating gravel, from which it gets minerals, salts, and grit to grind up seeds it eats. Moves in large flocks in winter. Sheds outer layer of its bill in spring, exposing blue green bill. More numerous in some years than others.

EASTERN MEADOWLARK
Sturnella magna

YEAR ROUND
SUMMER

Size: 9" (23 cm)

Male: A robin-shaped bird with brown back, lemon yellow chest and prominent black V-shaped necklace. White outer tail feathers.

Female: same as male

Juvenile: same as adult

Nest: cup, on the ground in dense cover; female builds; 2 broods per year

Eggs: 3-5; white with brown markings

Incubation: 13-15 days; female incubates

Fledging: 11-12 days; female and male feed young

Migration: complete, to Central America

Food: insects, seeds

Compare: The only large yellow bird with black "V" mark on chest.

Stan's Notes: A bird of open grassy country. Best known for its wonderful song. Often seen perched on a fence post, it will quickly dive into tall grass when approached. Has conspicuous white markings on each side of its tail, most often seen when flying away. Nest is sometimes domed with dried grass. Called "Meadowlark" because it's a bird of meadows and sings like the Larks of Europe. Not a member of the lark family, it actually belongs to the blackbird family. Related to blackbirds, grackles, and orioles. Hard to tell apart from Western Meadowlark except for song. Eastern's song is flute-like, clear, and a higher whistle compared to Western's lower, throaty call. Western is paler yellow and grayer than Eastern.

HELPFUL RESOURCES:

Beautiful Beachcombers Shorebirds. Morris, Arthur. Minocqua, WI: Northword Press Inc., 1996.

Birder's Handbook, The. Ehrlich, Paul and Dobkin, David S. and Wheye, Darryl. New York, NY: Simon and Schuster, 1988.

Birds Do It, Too, The Amazing Sex Life of Birds. Harrison, George and Kit. Minocqua, WI: Willow Creek Press, 1997.

Birds of Illinois, Bohlen, David H., IN: Indiana University Press, 1989.

Birds of Forest, Yard, & Thicket. Eastman, John. Mechanicsburg, PA: Stackpole Books, 1997.

Cardinal, The. Osborne, June. Austin, TX: University of Texas Press, 1995.

Chicago Area Birds, Mlodinaw, Steve., Chicago Review Press, 1984.

Cry of the Sandhill Crane, The. Grooms, Steve. Minocqua, WI: NorthWord Press Inc., 1992.

Dictionary of American Bird Names, The. Choate, Ernest A. Boston, MA: The Harvard Common Press, 1985.

Everything You Never Learned About Birds. Rupp, Rebecca. Pownal, VT: Storey Publishing, 1997.

Field Guide to the Birds, A: A Completely New Guide to All the Birds of Eastern and Central North America, Peterson, Roger Tory, and Virginia Marie Peterson. Boston: Houghton Mifflin Co., 1998.

Field Guide to the Birds of North America. National Geographic Society. Third Edition. Washington, D.C.: The National Geographic Society, 1999.

Folklore of Birds. Martin, Laura C. Old Saybrook, CT: The Globe Pequot Press, 1996.

Guide to Bird Behavior, Vol I, II, III. Stokes, Donald and Lillian.Boston, New York: Little, Brown and Company, 1989.

How Birds Migrate. Kerlinger, Paul. Mechanicsburg, PA: Stackpole Books, 1995.

Lives of Birds, The: Birds of the World and Their Behavior. Short, Lester L. Collingdale, PA: DIANE Publishing, 2000.

National Audubon Society: North American Birdfeeder Handbook. Burton, Robert. New York, NY: Dorling Kindersley Publishing, 1995.

Raptors, North American Birds of Prey. Snyder, Noel and Helen. Stillwater, MN: Voyageur Press Inc., 1991.

Secret Lives of Birds, The. Gingras, Pierre. Toronto, Canada: Key Porter Books Limited, 1997.

Secrets of the Nest. Dunning, Joan. Boston, MA: Houghton Mifflin Co., 1994.

Southern Illinois Birds, Robinson, Douglas W., IL: Southern Illinois University Press, 1996.

Stokes Bluebird Book: The Complete Guide to Attracting Bluebirds. Stokes, Donald and Lillian Stokes. Boston: Little Brown Co., 1991.

Stokes Field Guide to Birds. Eastern Region. Stokes, Donald and Lillian. Stokes Boston: Little, Brown and Company, 1996.

Stokes Purple Martin Book. Stokes, Donald and Lillian. Boston, MA: Little Brown Co., 1997.

For reporting unusual bird sightings or to hear a recording of where birds have been seen.

Chicago 847-265-2118

Dupage County 630-406-8111

Central Illinois 217-785-1083

Northwestern Illinois (Rockford) 815-965-3095

WEB PAGES:

The Internet has become a valuable place to learn about birds. The following are a few web sites that will assist you in your pursuit of birds. You might find birding on the net a fun way to learn more about birds or to spend a long winter night.

SITE	ADDRESS
Illinois Ornithological Society (IOS) PO Box 931, Lake Forest, IL 60045	http://www.chias.org/ios
Dupage Hotine site	www.gadwall.com/birding
Dupage Birding Club site	www.xnex.com/~ugeiser/ birds/birdclub.html
Illinois Natural History Survey Web Page	http://www.inhs.uiuc.edu
Chicago Audubon Society	www.audubon.org/ chapter/il/chicago
Chicago Birding Guide	www.gadwall.com/birding/ guide/index.html
Author's home page	www.naturesmart.com

CHECK LIST/INDEX

Use the boxes to check the birds you've seen.